DIGITAL
MISSIONARY

DIGITAL
MISSIONARY

FULFILL THE GREAT COMMISSION
WITHOUT LEAVING YOUR KEYBOARD

ANTHONY F. RUSSO

WORDS OF APPRECIATION

"Even if you do not think of yourself as a writer, you are." This simple truth sets the stage for *Digital Missionary*. Anthony Russo calls every believer to be cognizant of how they already transform their thoughts into written words—emails, social media posts, etc.—and then, to focus that process, that energy, into intentionally putting gospel truths into writing.

In this digital age, Christians are uniquely able to communicate biblical truth widely and, in the process, both evangelize the lost and to disciple fellow believers. While the book largely focuses on book writing, Russo notes that the principles apply to all forms of communication. The point is simply this: Use every available resource to propel the truths in your heart toward service to the King and His Kingdom.

The resources have changed over time; the (Great) commission has not. *Digital Missionary* challenges believers to love God and love people with words, written and disseminated, that others might be drawn nearer to the Savior in worship and adoration.

Steve Curtis, DMin, PhD
Founder and International Director
Timothy Two Project International, timothytwo.org

In *Digital Missionary*, Anthony Russo motivates the reader in a practical and encouraging way about how to become involved with publishing to minister to people around the world. He practically explains the impact publications can have both now and into the long-term future. It is a helpful book about how to impact lives for Jesus.

Anne Dryburgh, PhD
Missionary, Author, Professor

Here's a book that checks three critical boxes for those who long to see Christ made known among the nations. First, it's challenging. God has put it within His people to respond to a challenge. We feel the weight and glory of William Carey's challenge to expect great things from God and attempt to great things for God. *Digital Missionary* rings that bell.

Second, it's motivating. In this book, Anthony Russo leaves no room for doubt in the hearts and minds of those who have any inkling that publishing Christ abroad through books, pamphlets, and other digital means is a prolific way that God has chosen to advance the gospel. I want to be part of that!

Third, it's doable. There is no special talent required other than to say it the way you say it. Preach the word! Write it down! Send it forth! God will put it in front of those who need to hear it the way you say it for years and years to come.

J. Paul Dean, DMin
Pastor, Randall House Church, Greer, South Carolina

My friend, Anthony Russo, once again has a book balanced by Scripture and practice! A genuine read of the book will greatly inspire you to glorify God in your writing!

Johnny Touchet
Executive Director, Partner 10:15, partner1015.org

How beautiful upon the mountains are the feet of him who brings good news, who publishes peace." But what does it mean to publish peace? That is one of the questions Anthony Russo seeks to answer in Digital Missionary, which may be the first entry into a much-needed "Theology of Publishing" for the twenty-first-century Christian.

Skillfully applying the classic Protestant understanding of vocation to a variety of modern questions and situations that arise in our increasingly digital world, Russo presents an argument for why Christians ought to publish their perspectives far and wide. If you have thoughts, a pulse, and want to glorify the Lord of the gospel, this book is well worth your time.

Tony Arsenal, MA
Host, The Reformed Brotherhood Podcast

Dedications and Thanks

To all the saints who have mentored me by their words, written or spoken. I look forward to the day I get to thank each of you in person.

Thank you to Dr. J. Paul Dean for his helpful explanation of evangelism as "gospelizing" and for his continuing encouragement, pastoral leadership, and friendship. Thanks also to the elders and members of Randall House Church in Greer, South Carolina. "I thank my God every time I remember you. In every prayer for all of you, I always pray with joy, because of your partnership in the gospel from the first day until now" (Phil. 1:3-5).

Thank you to Cindy Agbenohevi for your early reader insights which were so helpful to smooth out so many rough edges. And, once again, special thanks to my two biggest encouragers: Jim Holmes at GreatWriting.org and my wife, Amy. Here we go again.

CONTENTS

Foreword 14

Creativity, Publishing, and the Glory of God 16

The Power to Publish 34

The Power to Proclaim 50

The Power to Save 64

The Power to Influence 78

The Power to Reach 94

The Power to Heal 110

The Power to Partner 122

The Power to Tear Down and Build Up 134

The Power to Lift Up 146

Conclusion: The Power to Serve 158

About the Author 168

Any Christian has a right to disseminate the gospel who has the ability to do so; and more, he not only has the right, but it is his duty to do so as long as he lives.

Charles Spurgeon

So the man went away and began to proclaim throughout the Decapolis how much Jesus had done for him. And everyone was amazed.

Mark 5:20

Foreword

I have known Anthony Russo for over five years. We have shared long conversations, deeply probing each other's ministries. I have been a guest on his podcast. Together, we raised funds for a young man, a double amputee suffering in a remote Ugandan village. We disseminated the young man's story throughout social media. We flew him to the US, arranged for state-of-the-art prosthetic treatment. We sent the young man to med school in Kampala. Anthony and I visited the young man's family in Africa, but separately, on different occasions. We have had, Anthony and I, an effective friendship and powerful collaboration in Christian ministry.

Yet we have never met. Not in person. Not even once. We have done all this remotely, using words alone, though not spoken words, the kind that resonate from vocal cords to human ears. Rather, our words have consisted of zeros and ones, engineered through bits and bytes, transmitted through pings and packets. We've used Zoom meetings, emails, WhatsApp, IMs, digital recordings, and other wonders of the electronic age to advance God's kingdom.

How apt, therefore, is Anthony's new book—*Digital Missionary*. Not only has he written it, he has lived it.

BRIAN ARNOLD, Founder and Executive Director, Grace-Bound.org
April 16, 2024

1

Creativity,
Publishing,
and the
Glory of God

In the apostle Paul's first letter to the Corinthians he exhorts them, **"So whether you eat or drink or whatever you do, do it all to the glory of God."** (1 Cor. 10:31). That phrase, "whatever you do," is joyfully wide open, isn't it? The only activities in all of life that are off-limits are sinful ones that would not glorify God.

In his booklet *Art & the Bible*, Francis Schaeffer suggests that David, as a young shepherd out in the pastures with flocks, composed his songs for his own enjoyment, but also as an act of worship.[1] Schaeffer makes the case that when Christians create art, it, too, can be both for the pure enjoyment of it, but also as an act of worship.

Thus, to paraphrase the apostle's words, *Whatever you design, build, clean, create or publish, whatever you do, do all to the glory of God.* This book is your invitation to publish for Jesus, or as I call it, to be a digital missionary: Use technology to create and publish for Jesus. Create what? That is up to you. It can be a blog, a podcast, a devotional,

1 Francis A. Schaeffer *Art & the Bible* InterVarsity Press. Downers Grove, Illinois, 1973. Page 24.

a song, posts on social media, videos, a book about your ministry, a novel, a cookbook, or even a math textbook. Apply all you know about your subject, do it thoughtfully and with excellence, work in the gospel or related biblical truth, and do it to the glory of God. Write and publish and create whatever God may be leading you to, for the sheer joy of doing it and as an act of worship. Get your message out to the world. Reach the lost, equip the saints, delight in the creative process, and worship the Lord like David did.

Developing a Theology of Publishing

If you and I are going to be digital missionaries, doing our part to fulfill the Great Commission through the creative gifts God put inside us, we need to take some time and think through what that means. Let me illustrate my point and then I think that will help explain where I am going.

When I first started my career in Information Technology (back when dinosaurs roamed the earth in search of a decent cell signal), I read a lot of books about technology so that I could be knowledgeable and apply what I learned. Eventually, I got a job using that knowledge to provide technical support to others. When I knew I wanted to be a writer, I read a lot of books on writing because I wanted to be knowledgeable about how to write well and communicate my ideas clearly to others. Then, when the Lord saved me, I began to read the Bible in earnest and a lot of other Christian books because—you guessed it—I needed to grow in my faith and knowledge because I wanted to please God and serve others.

Over my years as a Christian, I have been blessed by

many excellent Christian books. But to be honest, I have also read countless books and blogs, and heard podcasts and songs by professing Christians, that were terrible. Usually this happens because of bad theology, bad motives, or both. They publish a book that, frankly, would've been better for that book if it had it not been born. As Christians, we can and must do better, for the glory of God, as well as other reasons we'll get to.

In order for us to get the *right* message out the *right* way, so we can most effectively serve others, we need to develop a *theology of publishing*. And by "publishing," I do not mean solely books and printed media. Merriam-Webster defines "publish" as "to make generally known" or "to disseminate."[2] That is what writers and podcasters do: we "make generally known" our ideas, "disseminating" them to others.

What, then, is a theology of publishing? As Christians, we have a theology about everything, whether we realize it or not. As R.C. Sproul puts it, "Everyone is a Theologian."[3] Having a theology about a topic is to ask, *What does God think about a subject, and how then should we think and live in response?* Having a theology of suffering will aid you in understanding your trials in life and grow your faith in God to bring you through them. Paul was giving the Corinthians a theology of food when he advised them about meat sacrificed to idols and how it related to Christian liberty. Hence, one purpose of this book is that we want to arrive at a theology of writing and publishing, asking and answering the question: *What does God think about pub-*

---

2   https://www.merriam-webster.com/dictionary/publish.
3   It's not just Christians. Every human being has some theology (some developed ideas about God), as passages like Psalms 14 and 53 and Romans 1 teach us.

lishing, and how, then, should we publish in response?

It might surprise some to realize that God thinks about publishing. Along with everything else in creation, God gave us words. Along with words He gave us the idea to publish our words and ideas, and to invent the means to do that. (In fact, we need to recapture our sense of awe about how He has given *our* generation the ability to publish our words like none other has ever had!) God not only thinks about publishing, but He has also published—He gave us *the* Book! There are many references to words and publishing in Scripture, too many for us to cover here, but consider these words He inspired Isaiah to write (and publish!):

> **How beautiful upon the mountains are the feet of him who brings good news, who publishes peace, who brings good news of happiness, who publishes salvation, who says to Zion, "Your God reigns." (Isa. 52:7, ESV)**

Hopefully, I have given you food for thought toward answering the question, *What does God think about publishing?* As you read through the Scriptures you will notice (if you haven't already) the many passages about words and languages and writing and publishing. After a while, they will seem to leap off the page!

For the rest of this book we will think through the second part of the question: Since God is obviously interested in publishing, and in us publishing, how, then, should we publish in response?

Even if you do not think of yourself as a writer, you

are. You write emails. You write texts witnessing to unsaved friends or sharing counsel to brothers and sisters in Christ who are going through tough times. You write posts on social media. You write far more (and probably far better) than you think you do.

You also have dozens of conversations every week. Whether you realize it or not, you *are* a skilled communicator. Yes, others may be more gifted, but you can certainly use these everyday skills you have for Jesus. And like anything else, the more you do it, the better you will get. All of us communicate, so we need to be able to do that well, and part of that is using words well.

Did you know that when Solomon wrote Ecclesiastes, he was very careful about the words he chose? **"The Teacher searched to find delightful sayings and to record accurate words of truth,"** (Eccl. 12:10). Solomon's wise words are a master class in writing in a single sentence. Want to be a better writer? Be intentional to search out delightful sayings and thorough to record accurate words of truth. In short: Engaging words. Accurately written. Proclaiming truth.

Words are gifts God gave us to communicate with one another. Words *are* delightful. They are beautiful. Like flowers in a meadow, they vary in size, in bloom, in color, and in fragrance. They are gifts from God and colors for your palette. Delight in them. Pick them. Use them!

The Lord also used words when He wanted to communicate to us. He told us all we need to know about Him and salvation through words, first spoken and then written (2 Tim. 3:16). Jesus Himself is the Word, the full and final revelation of God to the world (John 1:14; Heb. 1:1).

So yes, words are important. How important? I am not exaggerating when I tell you that I rewrote this paragraph some twenty or thirty times because the words were never quite right. Never quite as delightful or engaging as I wanted them to be for you to read. However, don't be discouraged by my confession. If anything, it should motivate you. What I am saying by way of encouragement to you is this: *You don't have to know how to write great sentences to write a great book.*

Before this chapter ends, I want us to also consider one more topic, but before we do, I want us to look back at how much ground we've covered so far. Already we have touched on a theology of creativity, which led us to think about what it means to publish. That, in turn, helped us define what a theology of publishing is. Then we considered a theology of words to plug into our developing theology of publishing.

How versus Why

As you probably figured out by now, this is not a how-to book. I am not going to teach you how to write a sentence, how to acquire an agent, or how to sell a million books. . . Besides, "How" questions are, by nature, mechanical, the means to the end of something: Look it up. Find the answer. Do the thing. Move on. *How* questions about writing, publishing, podcasting, etc., can easily be answered by taking a class, reading an instructional book, or looking it up on YouTube. For the benefit of some readers, the last part of this chapter covers the fundamental steps of how to write and publish for Christ. If you're interested in that, I hope you find it helpful. If it does not apply to your situation, feel free to skim or skip it entirely; I won't be offended (well, maybe a little). In Chapter 2 and throughout the rest of the book we are going to get to *the good stuff*—the arguably *more important* stuff: The *Why*. Why it all matters.

It has been my observation that far too many professing Christians who write and publish focus on all those questions about *how* to write, *how* to build a platform, *how* to get an agent, *how* to submit a manuscript, *how* to get published, but they never really think (or think long enough) about the *why*.

We Christians need to be focusing on the Why of it all. *Why* is my idea important? *Why* is the ministry God has called me to lead important? *Why* am I so passionate about it? *Why* should my readers be passionate about it? *Why* should they tell their friends about it so *they* can get passionate about it too? In short, *why* bother? Answering *Why* is central to developing one's theology of publishing.

So, we are not going to spend a lot of time answering the *How* question, but rather the *Why* question: Why write and publish for Christ? Why be a digital missionary?

The short answer is: Because publishing for Christ has power. A lot of power. Not power from us, but from the Lord and for His glory. Publishing a book still has great potential.

Speaking of publishing a "book". . . Before we go any further, I have two notes and two apologies for you.

First, I am a writer. Most of my illustrations and much of this book will sound like I am only talking about writing and publishing books. I am not. I also podcast some.

I want to do more with audiobooks. My point is this: Although I talk mostly about writing and publishing books, the principles in this book apply to other digital missionary projects like blogs, podcasts, audiobooks, songs, etc. Feel free to apply the principles to whichever you are passionate about.

At the same time though, let me also add that I will be an unashamed advocate of writing and publishing books in particular. Podcasts and blogs are great resources in their moment, but they simply do not have the same enduring power that a traditional book (in any format) has. You may disagree, and I respect that. All I ask is that by the time you finish this book, you will at least consider reworking your best blog posts or podcast episodes to publish them in book form. Fair enough?

Second, being a digital missionary is to publish for Christ. I will use those terms interchangeably throughout the book. More often than not, when you see me use the word "publish," think of it in the broader application we discussed earlier.

As for my two up-front apologies: First, I apologize if too many of my examples draw from global missions and missionary biographies. I love reading about both. Beethoven and Handel both published for Christ, but I don't mention their contributions or examples because I don't move in those circles. Feel free to draw from your own areas of interest when thinking through and applying the principles throughout.

Second, this book focuses almost exclusively on writing and publishing adult nonfiction. If this is not your genre, please forgive me and seek to apply the principles to fiction, if that is your preferred genre. Since nonfiction is most near and dear to me, I can only write from what I know.

I know that quality Christian fiction can be God-glorifying. And I know it is more than romance stories and horse and buggies clopping along the road through Amish farmlands. I am just not well-read enough to talk at length about fiction's ability to glorify God. Although, of what little Christian fiction I have read, Daniel Defoe's *Robin Crusoe* was life-changing for me. I often reflect on his powerful imagery and riveting storytelling. And Bunyan's masterpiece is, well, Bunyan's masterpiece. I enjoyed C.S. Lewis' classic *The Screwtape Letters*. The only modern Christian fiction I have read was a trilogy of novels twenty years ago when I was a new Christian. The theology in them was broadly appealing, like popular Christian radio, but they were clean, whimsical fun.

So, while this book will focus on publishing nonfiction, the principles apply across all genres. I don't think you will be bored. We will have plenty to discuss. You may just need to think about it and decide who you are and what kind of book you want to write and publish. Or maybe you already know. (If so, great!)

I will only add that some genres either are automatically off-limits to believers or ought to be, as Scripture's command in Paul's words in Philippians makes clear.

Finally, brothers, whatever is true, whatever is honorable, whatever is right, whatever is pure, whatever is lovely, whatever is admirable—if

> **anything is excellent or praiseworthy—think on
> these things.**
> (Phil. 4:8)

Personally, I question how Christian romance novels glorify God, or why a Christian would want to write about a zombie apocalypse, or how that is in any way edifying to the Body of Christ. I cannot remember who pointed this out to me, but romance novels fill heads with a fantasy land, and only stoke discontented pining for what the reader does not have, causing one to grumble against God's providences in one's real life. And filling readers' minds with images of gore and decay, well, that seems obviously unedifying. You may disagree, but Philippians 4:8 sets clear guidelines for us as Christians.

Maybe you are reading this because you know you want to write something but are not sure what. That's fine, too. Pray about it as you read. To give you some ideas: A pastor can publish a sermon series that was especially helpful to his congregation. A missionary can write a book about his or her experiences, or to challenge the next generation to answer the call to world missions. Laypersons can write a memoir of God's dealings in their lives, to give help and hope to their readers. There are books and subcategories on all the major topics of Christianity: Church History, evangelism, missions, ecclesiology (the Church), theology, life problems and choices (career, marriage, singleness, parenting, grief, joy. . .). I assure you that you will have far more choices of topics to write about than years to do it.

Nuts, Bolts, and Bogs

As we begin to consider the *how*, the rest of this chapter is mostly mechanical, the nuts and bolts as they say. It contains the how-to side of this book. In another couple of pages, it's going to sound like a bunch of those nuts and bolts being shaken about in a wooden box. There are countless books about the art and mechanics of writing. No single book can cover every aspect, nor will this one. I will try not to get us bogged down in the details, but it's a bog that is impossible to avoid completely.

Once *un-bogged*, the rest of the book moves steadily through considering the *Why* of publishing for Christ. The last chapter, the conclusion, is where we take one final look back at our time together and hopefully by then you have been praying and are ready to find your place in the world of publishing for Christ. It is my prayer for you that you will commit to take advantage of the remarkable, powerful, gospel opportunity He has providentially given us in this era of Church history.

(Another bit of encouragement: You won't find "un-bogged" in the dictionary; but that's the beauty of writing and publishing; you don't have to follow *all* the writing rules from back in school, just most of them. Don't like any of your choices in the dictionary? As a writer, you can make up words!)

Ask new writers who their book is for, and they will almost always give the same disillusioned answer: *Everyone!* Yes, selling eight-billion copies of your book would be great (and a nice royalty check), but that's just not realistic. In marketing terms, you need to define your demographic—the composite picture of your ideal reader.

For example: Say you wrote a book for new Christian mothers. That automatically rules out half the world's population as potential buyers and readers. Nothing is wrong with that, it's just reality. In the same realistic way, a woman is unlikely to curl up with a book of reflections from spending many hours enjoying the beauty of God's creation while perched in deer stands and duck blinds. She might, but for that book, you will be more likely to attract the new dads.

You must select your audience, but at the same time I recommend you try to write to the ear of everyone. Going back to the example of a book for mothers, are you writing to expectant mothers? New mothers? Mothers of teens? Whatever season of motherhood you are writing to, write broadly within that category. Be thoughtful to write to all the moms in that season, regardless of cultural, economic, or educational background.

For myself, I mostly try to write broadly, with both men and women in mind. I think of people I know, young and old. Would they benefit from what I am writing? Would they connect with how I am writing it? If they passed my book along to a friend, would the friend benefit from the time invested to read it? I wrote this book for Christians, but I also wrote knowing God may choose to put it into the hands of non-Christians.

To me, that kind of forethought behind writing is biblical. It's a desire to love and serve readers. It is trying to be a Solomon, carefully choosing delightful words to present truth in a way that benefits anyone who reads them. It is also my small attempt to follow the apostle Paul's example, becoming "all things to all people, so that by all

possible means I might save some" (1 Cor. 9:22). I know "all people" won't buy my books, but stylistically I try to write them to serve anyone—hoping they come to know the Lord, if they don't already.

Point being: Smart publishing involves some strategy. You need to think about who is most likely to respond positively to your book. Not to sound crass about it, but: *Aim for their heart and mind with your writing and aim for their wallet with your cover and marketing.* Make the cover design attractive and then craft the book blurb (the brief description) to pique interest. I know. I don't like marketing gimmicks, but part of this is no gimmick at all; it is simply appealing to human nature. That said, never be worldly in marketing. For myself, whenever I have tried to market one of my books, I always made it about *the book*, not the author. I believe in *the book*. I believe it can be a helpful Christian resource for those I wrote it for, so I try to convey its value to be exactly that.

Here we come to the process of getting your book written and published. Contrary to the scores of books that claim otherwise, writing a book is not as easy as "1-2-3". It's more like as "easy" as 1-2-3. . . and all the way up to 10, or maybe 10,000. In short, it isn't all that short. Generally, the steps to publish a book are:

1. Come up with an idea big enough to be broken out into several smaller ideas; those will likely be the chapters comprising your Table of Contents.
2. Write a chapter or two, or keep going and write it all.
3. Decide on a publisher/publishing path (traditional or self-published).

4. If hoping for a traditional publisher, shop your idea around.
5. Write your book if you haven't already.
6. Work with your editor to rewrite and polish.
7. Design your book cover.
8. Give your manuscript to "beta-readers" to critique.
9. Incorporate relevant beta-reader suggestions.
10. Publish your book(*).

(*) In truth, Step 10 is not the end. In fact, it's only the beginning. Steps 11 through 10,000 all involve marketing and promoting your book for the foreseeable future, but only if you're focused on sales.

If you're writing a book for your ministry, you might be marketing and selling that book for the next twenty years as the centerpiece of your ministry. Or you may not do any marketing because you are only interested in writing and publishing a book of family history and recollections for your grandchildren (and their grandchildren!) to have after you are gone. But even then, you may find that others might be interested in reading your historical family memoir. That is one of the many rewards of publishing: you never know who your audience might be or how far your book will travel.

Another bit of truth has to do with Step 5, Write Your Book. Here again is where I am going to differ from 99 percent of the How-To books out there. Many make it sound easy. It isn't.

Writing a book is like competing in the *Tour de France* in your head. It starts off exhilarating, becomes grueling midway through, and eventually you reach a point where you just hope to finish without getting too banged up.

Writing is hard work. Why do you think something like 70 percent of people say they would want to write a book, but never actually do? There simply is no shortcut to it. There are no eBikes whisking riders effortlessly through the stages in the *Tour de France*. If there were, we would all be riding in it. It all comes down to self-discipline, effort, and perseverance.

The closest we writers get to eBiking our way through the Pyrenees of book writing are options like transcribing audio or hiring a coauthor or ghostwriter.[4] Those can certainly speed things along. A book is a journey of tens of thousands of words, written one at a time, and then many of them discarded and rewritten. And when you can't think of what else to write, you must wrestle through and keep writing.

Some might object to what I said above: "What about transcribing a sermon or narrating a book, or those other ways you mentioned?" Yes, those are options. But remember that the preacher did his heavy lifting on the front end, during the initial sermon preparation. Adam Smith, author of the seminal book on economics, *The Wealth of Nations*, stood at his fireplace and dictated his masterpiece to his scribe. Some may say, "Aha! See, easy!" Yes, easy for Adam Smith. Not so easy for his scribe transcribing it all in real time, by hand. Somebody down the line always has to do the work.

And, frankly, as much as I do not always enjoy the hard

---

4   A coauthor helps someone write the book and gets credited on the book as an author. A ghostwriter is someone hired to write the book anonymously, but your name goes on the finished product. Yes, this is the kind of thing you and I would have gotten a failing grade for in school, but in the publishing world—even the Christian publishing world—it is a common practice; I have already tipped my hand on the practice.

work of writing, I can tell you that you really do not want to take any shortcuts. It is worth the effort not to.

I am writing this in December in a coffee shop. Because I live in South Carolina and the winters are mild, the air conditioning is blowing cold today. It is freezing in here. My fingers are cold, making it hard to type. My hoodie is pulled up over my head. My word count so far is 6,986. My goal for this book is 25,000-30,000. I have a long way to go, but I also just crossed the 7,000-word mark, so I am officially around 20-25 percent done. A few more frozen coffee shop visits and a few more chocolate chip muffins and I will be done (I guess those are some other reasons I am not *Tour* material).

As someone once said, "I hate to write, but love to have written." For me, writing the first draft is the hardest part. Rewriting is the fun part. Designing the book cover is the exciting part. And that moment of holding your own hard work, neatly formatted and bound in your hands, is the best part, even if you never sell a single copy (which, honestly, really is highly unlikely).

But the freezing and pushing yourself to write, and then pushing yourself to persevere to the finish, are all part of the author experience. It is the difference between competing in the *Tour de France* and winning the yellow jersey, or just buying yellow jersey in a sporting goods store. Where's the thrill and adventure in that?

I will leave you with those thoughts on writing, otherwise this will become a book on writing, not publishing. But now you have a big-picture understanding of the process. For your book to be published, your book needs to be written. Writing and publishing a book is incredibly satisfying, but it takes work. There are ways to make it easier, but it still takes *somebody's* time, talent, and effort. There's no way around that, but that also means you can surround yourself with talented, experienced professionals to help you get you and your dream across the finish line.

Writing and publishing for Christ is entirely worth it. Having considered the *how to do it,* in the remaining chapters I hope to convince you of *why* it matters.

2

The Power
to Publish

It's 10pm. My wife has gone to bed without me. I am still awake. Still at my computer. Still typing. Off and on, I have been at my computer since around 7am, writing and rewriting. My eyes hurt and my brain can only focus on the sentence I am working on. Then the next one. Then the one after that. Must. Keep. Writing.

When I get into this kind of writing zone I eventually reach a good stopping point or my brain simply cannot form another coherent sentence, and I have let it go. Save a file. Walk away. Brush teeth. Go to bed exhausted, stiff, and yet in my head I am still trying to craft sentences. I let it go without realizing it. I have fallen asleep.

That is how I write. I do that nearly every day until I finish the rough manuscript. Once I get an idea and a general table of contents, I am a hermit. I try to take breaks. I think I am getting better at that, but probably not.

We can ask Amy when she wakes up.

Publish for Christ

Except for my quirky sleep-deprived hermit routine, I want you to write and publish a book. Or two. Or five. Let's start with one though. I will be happy with one, and so will you. And once you publish one, you will want to publish another. You heard it here first.

You may have noticed that I use the phrase *publish for Christ* instead of *Christian Publishing*. That is intentional. In my mind "Christian publishing" is too broad. Can we be honest and admit that there are some truly terrible books published in the world of "Christian" publishing? This book is not a rant against Christian publishers. I am, however, against those books that get published with broad appeal but bad theology, books where it is blatantly obvious the publisher had no desire to exercise any discernment whatsoever and is literally banking on their readers not to either.

Instead, I want to stir Christians to see the need, see the potential, and answer the call to write God-honoring, solidly biblical Christian books. Books that reach the lost with the gospel and build up the Body of Christ.

Any Christian can publish. I am urging you to publish *for Christ*.

Consider what we said earlier about what it means to publish. At its core, publishing is to make public. It is communicating a message. But that is only part of it. It's communicating a message to be *received* by others. To be *understood* by others. And it's communicating a message to *stir others to action*. I have already told you the result I am praying for: I want to inspire you to write and publish a theologically sound quality Christian book (or resource), to the glory of God. I am hoping to mobilize you and thousands like you to become digital missionaries, fulfilling the Great Commission through writing and publishing!

The message a writer chooses could be his or her own or someone else's message. As Christians, our message is ultimately not *our* message but God's. If we are writing something specifically Christian in subject, our message is wrapped up in God's message: The Good News of Salvation through the Son of God made Man, the Lord Jesus Christ. And if it's not, something is off in our message.

We write because we have a message, and so we aim to communicate that message in as compelling a way as possible, so it connects with our readers. We want them to receive our message, understand it, embrace it, and ideally to act on it. Some writers want to provoke their readers to their own level of outrage about a perceived injustice. Others only want to share their enthusiasm about a hobby, such as teaching readers how to tie fly fishing knots and sharing stories about the simple joys of fishing for trout. For myself, I want lost people to repent and be saved; and I want saved people to know, love, and serve the Lord even more.

I am guessing you are reading this book because you have a message in you that you want to share with others. What is that message? And what action do you hope your readers will take after reading your book? Do you want to help them solve a problem in their life? Do you want them to be excited about what God is doing in your ministry and become financial partners? Do you want dads to spend more time with their kids? Churches to be more thoughtful in how they minister to those with physical or mental difficulties? Or maybe you just want to write a lighthearted book to entertain readers. The world could always use more of those.

A gospel tract aims to compel its reader to repent and believe the gospel. A counseling book aims to give biblical hope to produce biblically informed change in the reader's heart. Both examples hope to convince the reader to shift from one conviction or position to another, maybe from ambivalence to action.

At the risk of overstating it, my aim for this book is to convince you of the incredible opportunity at your fingertips to write and publish something for the glory of God and the good of others. I have already said that I believe all of us are writers to some degree. I believe there is a book inside you. It may be a small book, but I believe it is there! But if writing is not your gifting, then find someone who wants to write and publish for Christ and help him financially get his book to the world. If one reader finishes this book and says, "All right. I'll do it!" and follows through, I will have hit my target.

Whatever your book idea is, publish to produce a change in your readers. Inspire them to fight sin. Help them grow in the Lord. Help them solve a problem. Show them why your ministry needs their help. The best books inspire change in their readers. It could be change of thought, a change of behavior, or both.

Every Christian a Publisher

Consider these words from Ernest Reisinger in his essay, *Every Christian a Publisher*: "The ministry of books can be used to evangelize, teach, train and expel ignorance as it has done in the past. . ."[5] Reisinger's words are compelling, and they are right. Every Christian should be actively involved in the power of publishing. But how?

Quality Christian writing requires the author to have solid biblical theology, self-discipline, a level of comfort with periods of isolation and, of course, the ability to write well. I would encourage any Christian who has even an ounce of those qualities to publish something for the Lord. Use what skills you have, learning and growing as you progress in your craft.

After my father died, I inherited a couple of his guitars. I did not know how to play guitar before, except for a few chords, but last year I began to study and learn. Dad started around age ten and played for over eighty years. I will never live long enough to be the musician he was, but I can practice and get better than the musician I am today. A year later, I am amazed at my progress. I have already dabbled in writing rudimentary songs, if for no other reason than the fun of it.

Anyone can do the same with writing. Start where are you are. Write about what you are passionate about and what you know about. Do a little research about writing (*you are already reading this book, so kudos to you!*), practice, and you will get better. Chisel your rough ideas out of the marble, sand them down the best you can, and leave the final polish to a skilled editor. Besides, the more we

5 https://graceonlinelibrary.org/salvation/evangelism/every-christian-a-publisher-by-earnest-c-reisinger/

do a thing, the better we get at it. My first book took years to write the first draft. My fourth book took one week. This book is almost three times longer than that book and took me just sixteen days to chisel out the first draft. (Four passes later, I'm still sanding rough edges, but that's also the fun of it.)

I understand that not everyone is a writer. Not everyone is a missionary or pastor, either. If you lack the discipline or ability to write a quality Christian book but have the financial means to fund someone who does, then do that. Get behind what God is doing through that writer's gifting and help get the book published. By funding such a person's writing ministry, you are partnering in gospel work. Consider the example of Benjamin Franklin and George Whitefield:

Did you know that the United States $100 bill is one of only two bills that does not feature a US president on it? Pull out a $100 bill (if you are already an author, you undoubtedly have many of these lying around).[6] Staring back at you with his polite-but-distant gaze is inventor, writer, publisher, and all-around Founding Father, Benjamin Franklin. That is why $100 bills are sometimes colloquially referred to as "Benjamins."

Although he is perhaps most known for inventing bifocals and supposedly flying a kite in an electrical storm, Ben Franklin was also a gifted writer and publisher. Did you know that, although he was a deist himself, Ben Franklin self-funded and published the sermons of his friend, the great evangelist George Whitefield? Franklin

---

6   Just kidding. By the way, the other bill not to feature a U.S. president is Alexander Hamilton on a $10 bill, which also happens to be the bill most authors are better acquainted with.

was not born again, but he strongly believed that Whitefield's sermons were useful in promoting a good and decent society. Franklin's intentions may have been misguided, but God used him to publish the gospel message in Whitefield's sermons far and wide across the colonies.

You can take inspiration from Franklin's enterprising spirit. Take some of your *Benjamins* and be a "Ben Franklin" yourself with them and help fund the publication of the gospel message in someone else's writings.

You may be wondering, "Fund publishing? I thought writers don't pay to get published; they *get* paid to publish." Well, yes and no.

Publishing 101

It's no secret that publishing takes money. Traditional publishers take on much of the cost themselves in hopes to eventually make a profit. That risk/reward scenario is why they must be selective in their publishing choices.

But to borrow a picture of the past, the "Iron Curtain" of traditional publishing has fallen. Nowadays, anyone has the freedom and power to publish. The power truly is at the tips of anyone's fingers. Yes, the investment is on the front end, and the author typically covers the cost, but for a Christian, what is that compared to the eternal profits if done with the right gospel motives?

It's not just book publishing that is at our fingertips either. A person can decide to create a website, find a domain name, create a blog on any subject, and have it all up and running almost instantly. Getting readers is much harder, but the fact is this: Anyone can publish anything, and often within days, hours, or even minutes.

There are still traditional writing opportunities out there as well, for both staff and freelance writers. There are opportunities to write articles for Christian online journals and blogs all the way up to monthly devotionals for larger ministries, or doing copywriting, etc. The pay may not be great, if at all, but they are opportunities to hone your craft and build your writing portfolio.

You can publish exclusively eBooks, or print books, or both. Nowadays, the ability to do either is almost *too* easy (more on that in the next chapter). Whatever your genre, whatever your target audience, barring any of the obviously sinful literary genres, you can find a place to serve as a digital missionary and publish for Christ.

Personally, I have gone the self-publishing route so far. I have my own imprint (Mark520.org). You can, too. Or you can elect to submit your manuscript to traditional publishers. (I told you that you had options!)

If you are a ministry leader, publishing a book is a no-brainer. Every leader of a sizable church or a ministry of nearly any size ought to consider it. If God has given you that kind of influence, use it for Him. A book is also a great way to tell others about your ministry, like Richard Wurmbrand's story of his life in his book, *Tortured for Christ* (Voice of the Martyrs) or Brother Andrew's *God's Smuggler* (Open Doors).

A book is a great way to communicate with your donors or to alert others to what God is doing in the ministry and invite them to be a part of it. Again, more on that later.

Reality Checks

Before you dream about royalty checks I need to give you a few reality checks. Up to this point I have been intentionally optimistic. I want you to see the potential in publishing—the good it has done, can do, and how you can be involved. But I also need to be realistic with you:

First, writing and producing a book is hard, as we have already established, and will discuss more in the next chapter. It is why most people only dream of it, but never actually do it. Case in point:

The day I worked on the second-round rewrite for this chapter I saw a title on someone's LinkedIn profile that made me laugh and shake my head in disbelief at the silliness of it. Someone had the audacity to put on his LinkedIn bio (the few keywords that summarize who you are *and what you have done*) that he is an "aspiring author." What does that even mean? It isn't an accomplishment—it's a pipe dream. I might as well update my bio with "aspiring astronaut." I admit I am having a bit of fun at the pretentiousness so often on display on LinkedIn, but it validates what I said earlier: Writing a book is hard, and that is why most people only dream about, er, *aspire* to it.

Second, well, about those royalty checks. . . most self-published books do not sell well (although self-published fiction sells better than self-published nonfiction). Yes, you may spend all that time and energy to write, rewrite, edit, design, and publish your book, only to have it go nowhere. You will not get rich. You will not have Ben Franklin looking up and smiling at you when you open your wallet. In fact, you may sell only 100 or 200 copies and give away more copies than you sell. The whole gambit may be a losing proposition, humanly speaking. It can be discouraging. But you must encourage yourself in the words of C.T. Studd:

> 'Tis only one life, and soon will pass.
> Only what's done for Christ will last.

As we were in the final editing stages of this book my editor had lunch with another client of his. That brother told him how his own book hadn't sold very many copies either and that he, too, had given away more copies than he sold. When pressed for numbers, he said that he hadn't just given away a few thousand copies, but more like ten thousand! That brother knows that it isn't the royalty checks in this life that matter most. He's holding out for the deferred payment royalty check that has in the memo line, **"Well done, good and faithful servant! You have been faithful with a few things; I will put you in charge of many things. Enter into the joy of your master!"** (Matt. 25:23). Only what's done for Christ will last.

If God has given you the ability, and it is not taking away from your family budget or other priorities, so what if you spend a few thousand dollars to produce a quality book that is evangelistic to the lost or seeks to build up believers, never to recoup your money in this lifetime? The Lord who owns the cattle on a thousand hills can richly reward you for your humble writing effort in innumerable ways, either in this life or the next. There are also a number of other reasons I will get to as to why I still recommend you go for it.

Let me share my own writing and publishing results with you:

As of this writing (December 2023), I have published four books.

My first book, *Pleasant Places,* was a collection of devotional-type essays that were originally blog posts on an old blog. That book was published in 2014. So far it has sold well over a dozen copies—maybe even two dozen, but I don't want sound like I am bragging! When I first published it, I did not know that most devotional books don't sell well because the market is flooded with them; I just wanted to try to write a book for Jesus, and I did!

The second book was a kind of experiment. It was little business-genre $1.99 eBook I created. It was fun to put together, but a commercial flop because of my own ignorance.

My third book, *Jesus Changed Everything,* was an evangelistic book to give away to people. I wrote that in 2021. Here again, I don't mean to brag but that one has outsold my first book by almost double.

I wrote my fourth book, *Love, Lead, Serve,* this year (2023). I was invited to speak to pastors and seminary students as part a short-term mission trip to Africa. As I prepared my speaking notes, I figured rather than simply write up my notes and pass them out as stapled handouts, I would publish them as a small book and bring copies with me. It turned out to be a pleasant surprise for the attendees and "thank you" gift for my hosts. So, how has it done? I have given away most copies. I have sold almost no copies of that one at all.

Surprised?

What you need to understand is that I also did very little marketing for the first two books. For the evangelistic book, I started out of the gate strong and had early momentum but I did not keep the marketing machine going. I cranked it up and kind of walked away. When it sputtered and quit, so did my sales. And I did no marketing at all for the Africa book, not even a single post on Facebook to friends.

What is the moral of my story? My "sales" have always been *exactly in line* with my marketing, and yours probably will be too. No marketing = no book sales, period.

But that is the difference: I was okay with that. I genuinely do not want a "platform." I like to write and, yes, I like when others read my books, but I would rather sell no books and give away copies than present myself on social media and elsewhere as some expert, even on Christian things. The only thing I am on expert on is my own sin.

Let my story be your example, and perhaps your inspiration if you like. I am a nobody, just an ordinary Christian. But I can do a bit of writing, and I enjoy it, so I also enjoy investing the talents the Lord has entrusted to me into publishing, even if it means giving away more books than I sell.

Maybe one day I will sell more books; that would fun. I wouldn't complain. If you make the effort to market your book, you will almost certainly enjoy better sales, if that's what you want. And if you already have a ministry or already have an influence over many people, your book should do well with your audience. Just remember this: In your eagerness for sales, you may sell yourself short.

2124 and Beyond

You see, when it comes to publishing for Christ, it's not about immediate sales. In fact, it's not about long-term sales either. It's not even about sales in your lifetime. It's about doing what you do for the Lord and His glory. That can't be quantified on an Excel spreadsheet.

I love it when people read my books. I praise God for it. I pray God somehow uses my books to help them grow in their knowledge of Him, love for Him, and love and service of others. But I no longer write primarily for my generation. Now I also write for future generations.

When I first started, I only thought of the immediate and short-term timeframes. *Who will buy and read my book today or tomorrow?* At some point I had an epiphany. I realized my books will outlive me, and that made a profound difference on my perspective. Here is how my perspective changed:

I enjoy finding old books and articles online that have been preserved by being digitally scanned made available. I love to browse sites like ccel.org, monergism.org, archive.org, and biblicalstudies.co.uk. Every time I am on these sites, I find some obscure book, article, or even a short quotation maybe not even attributed to a particular person, but there it is, in a corner of some Christian evangelism or mission society newsletter from a hundred years ago or more.

One day, I realized that somebody took the time to write something God-honoring to serve Christ and His Church. And decades, or even a century later, here I come along and am edified by what that person wrote, someone who had no idea what he was writing might exist so far into the future. Imagine trying to explain to people like that how their work would one day be available instantly from just about anywhere in the world. Who could have imagined?

It's my hope that someday, somehow, if the Lord does not return before then, that in a hundred years or more, people might stumble across some preserved fragment of something *you* wrote, whether your name appears under it not. I want them to be strengthened in their faith as a result or, if they don't know the Lord, that He might use it in bring them to repent and believe. How great would that be! That is the power of publishing.

3

The Power
to Proclaim

When it comes to the gospel, most of us probably don't think of ourselves as "proclaimers." If you are like me, when I hear the word "proclaimer," I get the picture in my mind of a colonial-era town crier in a three-point hat, ringing a bell and holding open a scroll as he calls out, "Hear ye! Hear ye!" We may say we "tell" others about Jesus or "share" the gospel. We may even go so far as to say we "warn" sinners of their need to repent and believe the Good News. But to "proclaim" it? "No, not me," we say. "That's what my pastor does." Yet, proclaiming is exactly what we are doing.

In the New Testament, to proclaim is the Greek word "kerusso." It occurs over sixty times in the New Testament and it means to announce or proclaim. A similar word, "euaggeli[d]zó", is more specific. That word means to announce or proclaim *the gospel*, the Good News of salvation. The word literally means, "to gospelize." While it is true that, strictly speaking, the words refer to oral pronouncements of the message, publishing has within it the power to "proclaim" the Good News of salvation in written form.

Just consider the example of the humble gospel tract. These powerful little leaflets are sermons in miniature, proclaiming of the gospel of peace to guilty sinners. Gospelizing in black and white.

Envoys for Christ

In the Old Testament, God chose the prophets to be His envoys, declaring His message to individuals and nations. In the New Testament, Paul declares that God built the Church **"on the foundation of the apostles and prophets, with Christ Jesus Himself as the cornerstone"** (Eph. 2:21). And, of course, let's not forget that "apostle" means "messenger/sent one." You and I are not, nor can we be, "apostles" in the truest sense of the word. That office concluded when John, as the last living apostle, died. But as Christians, we have been commissioned as messengers, sent out from God to proclaim Him in the world (Matt. 28:18-20).

Recently I was meditating on Proverbs 13:17b, **"a faithful envoy brings healing."** An envoy is an ambassador, right? When the ruler is not there himself, he sends diplomatic envoys to represent him and deliver a message on his behalf. They are not delivering their own message or their own views. Rather, they are to faithfully communicate the message their ruler gave them to relay.

In 2 Corinthians 5:20, the apostle Paul refers to himself and his ministry companions as **"ambassadors for Christ, as though God were making His appeal through us. We implore you on behalf of Christ: Be reconciled to God."** The same principle applies to us. You and I are envoys of the King of Kings and Lord of Lords. It is our privilege to be trustworthy envoys for God, bringing His message of reconciliation to a lost and dying world.

One important point I mentioned in Chapter 2 is worth repeating here: As envoys, when we are publishing something Christian in nature, our message is not our own. The message we are to proclaim is the Lord's. It comes from His Scriptures. The gospel message we have is *authoritative*. It has authority because it is God's message, from God's Word, and God is the Authoritative Authority (if I can put it that way), over His whole universe.

There are two tempting ditches we must guard carefully against falling into. On one hand, we must turn away from any temptation to use the Word of God to churn out a "how to have a better life" book. Leave the pop culture gimmicks to the self-help prophets of Baal.

On the other side of the road, we must especially avoid claiming any supposed "new" message or new revelation from God. You would think this goes without saying, but over the years, professing Christians have published plenty of Christianized self-help, life-coaching type books and some have even had the audacity to make the heretical claim that their books were God speaking through them.

Such books only tickle itching ears with plausible arguments (Col. 2:4; 2 Tim. 4:3). A few may have sold millions of copies, but they are still lies bought and passed around by the undiscerning. I once met a man who handed out copies of one such book by the caseload. He lacked discernment. He intended good but he was unwittingly handing out evil.

We must also be careful not to sin like Elisha's servant,

Gehazi, did. He sinned in his covetousness and greed when he sought to profit from his position after he relayed Elisha's healing instructions to leprous Naaman (2 Kings 5). Here again, consider Paul's words in 2 Corinthians, **"For we are not like so many others, who peddle the word of God for profit. On the contrary, in Christ we speak before God with sincerity, as men sent from God"** (2 Cor. 2:17). Our motive must be God honoring.

Joy, Privilege, and Responsibility

At the same time, writing and publishing for Christ is a joy and a privilege. As Francis Schaeffer reminded us, there is a certain sense of art-for-art's-sake in the creative process. When I get going with arranging and rearranging words and ideas, it is satisfying in the same way it is satisfying for a woodworker to hole up in the workshop, amidst the smell of fresh cut wood and mounds of sawdust as his creation takes shape. Hours pass by as minutes.

We absolutely can and should delight in the act of writing, but if we are in any way teaching about the things of God or life, we must also have a healthy, holy fear about it, a respect for God and our readers.

Remember the story of Uzzah and the ark of God? In 2 Samuel 6:1-7 and 1 Chronicles 13:9-12, we read the story of how he reached out his hand and touched the holy ark of God to steady it as oxen stumbled and caused the ark to totter. Times have changed. The covenant we live under with God is different. But the Lord is the same. We must not trifle with how we handle the things of God.

Some might read this and dismiss me as being overly

dramatic or having an axe to grind. I am not and I don't. All of us must choose: Do we want to churn out "pulp Christian" that panders to the present pop Christian culture, or do we want to take the opportunity before us seriously, and write for a readership of One, if it came down to that? If we are to hold a proper theology of Christian writing and publishing, we must think of what we do as teaching, and Scripture has something to say about that, so we must heed its warning.

Writing and publishing Christian materials is a form of teaching. If I am writing and telling readers something about God—His Person, His attributes, etc.—or about us, or how the Bible addresses a certain issue and counsels us to live, how can that be anything other than teaching? And Scripture warns that teachers will be held to stricter judgment (James 3:1).

Just as any man who steps behind a pulpit to preach ought to do so with sober healthy fear and awe at the responsibility entrusted to him, we must not leap naively into writing and publishing for Christ. To put it bluntly: You and I will stand before God for what we tell others; we had better get our theology correct from the Scriptures and in accord with same truths that have been proclaimed for two thousand years of Church history.

Your Book as Your Altar

Recently I was reading again the story of Gideon, and something in his story stuck out to me as a lesson to myself about writing and publishing. I would like to share it with you:

Judges 6:24 says, **"So Gideon built an altar to the**

LORD there and called it The Lord Is Peace. To this day it stands. . ." As I meditated on that verse, I got to thinking about how, in a very real sense, all of us are spending our lives building an altar to something. Think about it.

Biographies are fascinating, aren't they? Entire lives are lived out in a few hundred pages. Some people invest this brief life in the Savior and enjoy dividends of eternal life and joy. Others, such as many (not all) Hollywood celebrities, athletes, business titans, and rock stars live as gods among men—almost. They have everything at their fingertips. Many squander their life in folly and excess. Some get to live long lives, while others die in their prime and leave us to wonder what would have been?

I think of this too whenever Amy and I watch old television shows. Lately we have been watching a few detective and private investigator shows from the 1970s and '80s. It's always amusing to me to see the old cars, the signs, and the fashions that were all once so trendy and cool, but now are laughably dated. But I am also struck by the leading actor. He or she was at the top of his or her career, living it up in Los Angeles, on TV every week and on and on. . . . Yet, now, he or she is old or dead. All the glitter and glam of that life is gone. Was it worth it?

I am not knocking those people. I am not judging them. I had my time in this world. I pursued what mattered to me and not to God. But then God intervened and saved me, an undeserving sinner, and for reasons known only to Him. My point is only to have us look beyond this brief life and reflect on eternity. We will be there infinitely longer than we are here. When we read the lives of others, and how they chose to live their lives—good or bad—how can we not contemplate our own lives? Which also brings us back to Gideon.

Gideon's altar is a lesson in metaphor for us all. All of us are passing our days building something. The parts (our days and our works) will equal a whole (our life), but what will the result be? What will it signify to those who remain after we are gone? To what, or to whom, are we dedicating our "altar"?

"Gideon built an altar to the Lord there and called it The LORD Is Peace. To this day it stands. . ." Godly Sunday School teachers erect an altar to the Lord, faithfully teaching children about Him. So do godly parents. Every Christian, in his own God-given way, leaves behind some testimony of the Lord and His goodness.

Have you ever considered writing a book as your "altar to the Lord"? A book is a tangible way you can leave your testimony about the LORD for your generation and beyond, an altar built not with stones but with words, erected for all to see so they would be moved to know, love, and serve the Lord Jesus Christ.

Thomas Jones said, "We must preach Christ because there's no other message from God." He is the glorious Subject of the message we are to proclaim. If you are wondering who Thomas Jones is, to be honest, I had no idea when I found the quotation. I found his words in an old book digitized and preserved on the Internet. It turns out that Jones (1841-1926) was one of the last of that famous band of men, the Methodist circuit-rider preachers. Jones served the Lord in Oregon for over half a century. I was blessed by what he wrote and now, as I include his words here, his godly advice speaks to a whole new generation one hundred years after his death as you and I discover them for ourselves. I do not agree with all the points of his theology in his writings, but his words here serve as a powerful reminder to us, and the "stumbled across them" way they came to be included in a book being published in 2024 reinforces the power and the potential of the published word.

We need to have a purpose in our lives greater than anything else, and that purpose must be to make God known, working for Him (Mal. 1:11). Make full use of the Power to Proclaim. Publish the Good News to sinners that God might use it to save them and publish it to saints so that God might refresh and strengthen them in the battle.

Proclaim Him to children through a Christ-exalting children's books if that is your area of ministry giftedness. Proclaim Him to teens and young adults to give them much-needed light from Scripture for their paths in the world. Proclaim Him to men and women in the prime of their lives, to provide godly wisdom, godly relaxation, godly help for their problems, and so on.

Provide words of comfort and companionship to those aged saints who are nearly done running their race. Tell the unsaved lonely widow who is a home-bound shut-in that she can be shut in the Ark, who is Christ. Comfort the Christian widow, reminding her that Jesus is with her every day, protecting her and providing for her needs. Encourage the dying saint, that they now share in the triumphs of the One who conquered fear and death and will soon have the joy of seeing Him face-to-face.

A Heart to Proclaim

Ask any preacher of the gospel, and he will tell you his heart often aches for his hearers. His message is Good News, but he also exhorts, encourages, and warns. Every book on preaching I have ever read inevitably speaks of the need for a preacher to fulfill his task with conviction, earnestness, urgency, and, above all, love. Our writings for the cause of Christ should reflect those same qualities. How can we accomplish this? Again, we can look to Jesus as our Wonderful Example.

Matthew tells us Jesus went about His ministry of preaching, teaching, and healing the people having **"compassion for them, because they were harassed and helpless, like sheep without a shepherd"** (Matt. 9:36). When He fed the five thousand, Matthew again notes that He **"had compassion on them"** (14:14). Feeding the four thousand, Jesus said to His disciples, **"I have compassion for this crowd"** (15:32; Mark 8:2).

In Mark's account of the feeding of the five thousand, he adds that same shepherding language: **"When Jesus stepped ashore and saw a large crowd, He had compassion on them, because they were like sheep without a shepherd. And He began to teach them many things"** (Mark 6:34).

In Luke's Gospel, he records the day a funeral procession went by Jesus and how a widow was weeping because now she had also lost her son. **"And the Lord having seen her,"** Luke writes, **"was moved with compassion on her and said to her, 'Do not weep'"** (Luke 7:13). I could go on and on with examples, and of course *everything* that Jesus did in His earthly ministry flowed from His blessed compassion.

To publish for Christ as a digital missionary, to preach His Good News, to be His envoy, we must have a compassionate heart and see people the way Jesus did. We write and publish *evangelistically* because we see lost humanity as we once were, as sheep without a shepherd. We write to help *to disciple believers* because we see them as we now are, as sheep in God's flock, but so prone to wander and injure ourselves that we constantly need to be led back to the safety of our Shepherd.

Do the Thing Which Will Last Forever

My brother shared an interesting story with me I think you will appreciate. His pastor wrote a song back in 1970. It was the only song he'd ever written. Because he is from India, he wrote it in his mother tongue, Hindi. Recently someone discovered his song, translated it into Tamil, and recorded it. Isn't that wonderful? Fifty-four years later, someone, somehow, finds his song and gives it new life, to a new generation, and in another language. That is the power of proclaiming when we answer the call to become a digital missionary and publish for Christ.

I grew up as a child of the 1970s. For some reason, I remember time capsules were kind of a fad. It seemed like the newspapers were always running stories of a box of mementos either being encased in the cornerstone of a new building or being dug out of an old one. For those who leave a time capsule to some generation in the future, there is some kind of wonder at the prospect of it, as if one could really touch and be part of the distant future. And there was always a sense of wonder and excitement when we, that distant generation our forebears only could imagine, can now break open those legacies found in a box. *What treasures might have been packed away by townsfolk from a generation or two ago?* As far as I can recall, the optimistic zeal always gave away to disappointment. All they ever seemed to find in those rusted-out containers believed to hold such promise were deteriorated fragments of old documents, ruined by years water intrusion, a few coins, and some amusing trinkets. Isn't that so like the things of this world? So full of promise, and yet so disappointing!

Contrast those corroded time capsules with storing up treasures in heaven, **"where moth nor rust do not destroy and where thieves do not break in and steal"** (Matt. 6:19-20). Wouldn't it be far more exciting to have someone be blessed when they discover *your* song, *your* book, *your* words fifty or a hundred years from now? Imagine your words being translated and proclaiming the excellencies of the Lord Jesus Christ to a whole new generation of people!

I am fascinated by the era of mid-late 1800s. It was an historic time for explorers, world missions, and evangelism. Giants walked the earth, men like David Livingstone, Charles Spurgeon, Hudson Taylor, and George Muller. There were godly women, too. Susannah Spurgeon was serving with her husband, young Amy Carmichael was just coming into her own, and an aged Fanny Crosby was actively penning her catalog of what would amount to over 8,000 hymns.

During this time, there were many Christian organizations known as "societies." One such group was founded by American Congregational minister Francis E. Clark.

In an address to "The Endeavorers" Christian Society, he borrowed the language of that modern marvel of the day, household electricity, to urge evangelistic zeal saying, "Let every one of us be a live wire to connect this world with God." How can you be a "live wire" for Jesus?

In one of the Society's books for young people, *Aids to Endeavor*, Clark quotes Scottish Baptist Alexander Maclaren, *Do the thing which will last forever*. What a powerful word!

One hundred years from now, when people look back at our still relatively new Internet age, what will they say? Think of the incredible advancements of the Industrial Age, both in society and for the furtherance of the gospel, and then multiply that ten-thousandfold for this Information Age. You have an incredible, unique opportunity living in this age that you do. How can you be a digital missionary and use the technology available to us today to advance the Kingdom?

May the words of those godly men burn in our hearts. May the examples of so many godly women, industrious for the Savior, inspire us. May we make full use the technology available to us today, harnessing this power to proclaim Christ and all His glorious excellencies—proclaim them loud and clear like we were town criers of the Internet Age!—that we might connect this world to God and do the thing which will last forever: Touch lives through publishing for Christ.

4

The Power
to Save

Thirty years ago, back in the early 1990s, I got called into work in the middle of the night. Driving the dark empty highway from Bordentown, New Jersey, to Princeton (the office was a couple miles north of the famous university), something big was glowing orange on the side of the road ahead in the distance. Getting closer, I saw it was a car on fire. I don't remember all the details anymore, but I remember stopping to help the driver.

About all I remember is that he was lying on the road outside the driver's side and his leg was hurt. He couldn't walk away to get a safe distance from the car. I was young enough at the time that I thought cars exploded like they do in the movies (they don't). I pulled him a safe distance away from the car, about twenty or thirty feet. I vaguely recall police showing up and I recall giving my information to a police officer for his report. With the driver safe and the situation under control, I headed into the office to deal with the late-night computer emergency that now seemed, by comparison, to be not nearly as important or exciting.

That was my one and only experience saving someone's life and, to be honest, to even call it that feels shamefully overstated. He might have been fine to get to safety without me. Either way, there was no real risk of injury to me at any point.

My little experience is nothing compared to an ordinary day in the life of a police officer, firefighter, Emergency Room doctor or nurse, or EMS first responder! These professionals and others like them have a valor gene in their DNA that most of the rest of us are missing. They devote their lives to saving others from sickness, pain, abuse, and death. Many serve in hostile, miserable, or dangerous conditions. Unlike that night on the highway for me, these people *do* risk their own lives to save others.

The ultimate example of the power to save is, of course, God's great kindness to save us underserving sinners. And then, after He does, He equips and empowers us through the Spirit to participate in His ongoing redemptive work around the world.

That's what this chapter is about—publishing's power to save and how *you* can write, publish, or support publishing to be used by God to reach the lost and rescue dying men and women.

Missionaries or Imposters?

Christians are to be about the business of advancing the Kingdom. Charles Spurgeon said, "Every Christian is either a missionary or an impostor." All of us are in what Paul called **"the ministry of reconciliation"** (2 Cor. 5:18). God places each of us in the callings He does so that we can carry out the good works He assigned to us (Eph. 2:10).

As we go about our lives and faithfully do our small part in fulfilling the Great Commission, the kingdom of God advances. Granted, it may not seem like it most of time. It can seem like nothing attempted for Christ has much impact. But it does. We just don't often see it. **"The wind blows where it wishes,"** Jesus said. **"You hear its sound, but you do not know where it comes from or where it is going. So it is with everyone born of the Spirit"** (John 3:8). When Christians are busy doing what Christians do, those seemingly ordinary acts are the Kingdom in quiet, steady advance; the Spirit, like the wind, blows into the lives of those He redeems.

Just as there are many different careers which have a power to save in a temporal way, there are also various roles God employs His children in to accomplish His plans. Oftentimes, I find that God uses their day-to-day work and career for remarkable gospel-specific purposes. I once met a brother who served as the chaplain of a field office of the United States Secret Service! What a reminder he was to me about how the Lord wisely ordains His people to represent Him in places you and I often never imagine. Another brother used the clever avoidance skills he learned in his prior life of covert military operations to aid underground Christians in a restricted nation.

Exciting as those two examples are, the Lord places most of us in more ordinary, everyday roles to do His work. Besides the calling of being pastors, God calls Christians to be Sunday School teachers, street evangelists, sidewalk counselors and evangelists in front of abortion clinics, and, of course, the vital God-given role of parents to evangelize their children in the home. He raises us up as accountants, software developers, tradespeople, daycare workers. . . and, yes, writers. He reaches out to seek and save the lost every day and uses His people—you and me—in the process. What a privilege to be part of His great work.

Writing and publishing for Christ is perhaps the second-greatest means available to reach the lost and make disciples, second only to preaching. With today's publishing technology and near-instant "to market" possibilities, anyone who wants to write and publish for Christ, can. Consider the following story.

A.W. Tozer wrote his famous *The Pursuit of God* on an overnight train. Remarkable, for sure, but it would have been impossible for him to have it formatted, typeset, get a cover designed, and make it available for sale around the world by the time the train pulled into the station the next morning.

But you can.

With today's publishing technology, you could pull a "Tozer," staying up all night writing a manuscript, and then publishing it for sale on Amazon's worldwide websites by breakfast, and potentially have your first sale by dinner. Granted, all of that is unlikely to happen at quite that pace. Few of us can write a manuscript in a night, and sometimes Amazon will have delays for file reviews and release dates. But the technology is already in place. In theory it could be done, which is something no other generation ever had the power to do. That is amazing potential for getting your gospel message out there!

Think of the urgent need that exists. How many friends and loved ones do you have who, unless the Lord intervenes and saves them, are a heartbeat away from an eternity in hell? How many neighbors and people in your town? I live in South Carolina, part of America's "Bible Belt" of Southern states, where it seems everyone who grew up here considers himself or herself a Christian almost by birthright. Just yesterday my wife and I had lunch in a restaurant with background music playing "Nothing but the Blood of Jesus" and other hymns on their overhead music system, and no one thought it strange or complained. That's life in the South. However, for all its love of "that old time religion" and its plethora of churches, the American South is actually dry land that is hardened against the seed of the gospel.

You may live in a place that is gospel-hardened for other reasons. The American northeast, the Mid-Atlantic, and New England states were once places of great spiritual revival, and home to some of the greatest Christian thinkers, preachers, and missionaries this country has ever seen. Now those regions are post-Christian. The great universities founded for the training of men for the advancement of the gospel have all been lost to theological and political liberalism. All that godly influence has been replaced by humanism, liberalism, or false religions. But people there still need Jesus!

Consider Jude's charge to his readers in verse 23 of his letter: **"Save others by snatching them from the fire; and to still others show mercy tempered with fear, hating even the clothing stained by the flesh."** Our lives are to be marked by fervent prayer and action. We are to be working and supporting efforts to compel men, women, and children to repent and believe the gospel and be disciples of Christ. That's why, no matter where we live, God calls us to be involved in Kingdom efforts. Publishing for Christ and supporting publishing efforts is a great way for you and me to be busy in the work.

In his *Evening by Evening* devotionals, Charles Spurgeon says this for the evening of December 17:

> We are called to bear witness to the truth, to cheer the discouraged, to warn the careless, to win souls, and to glorify God.

Spurgeon's words so apply to our discussion that they would easily deserve to be included in every chapter of this book. Publishing's usefulness to bearing witness, cheering, warning, winning, and glorifying God cannot be overstated. Publishing for Christ is an incredible Great Commission opportunity! More Christians need to see its potential and take advantage of it, whether by writing or by funding Christian publishing efforts. Surely there must be some booklet or book inside you? Pray, make a cup of coffee, and start writing!

Consider these words from Francis Schaeffer:

> Each generation of the church in each setting has the responsibility of communicating the gospel in understandable terms, considering the language and thought-forms of that setting.[7]

In other words, you and I have a responsibility to our generation to tell them about Jesus, and in a way that can

7   Francis A. Schaeffer, *Escape from Reason*, InterVarsity Press (2014 reprint), page 120

be understood, while being careful not to compromise the message. **"We do not use deception, nor do we distort the word of God,"** Paul told the Corinthians. **"On the contrary, by setting forth the truth plainly we commend ourselves to everyone's conscience in the sight of God"** (2 Cor. 4:2, NIV). When you write something that evangelizes and disciples others or when you support a publishing project that does, you are publishing for Christ. You are seizing upon the great opportunity to use today's technology for good and for God, to point others to Him.

You can make the most of the modern ease of publishing, leveraging it to fulfill Jude's charge to snatch others from the fire and show mercy when you

- Publish your book
- Record your book as an audio book
- License the translation rights
- Start your blog
- Build and maintain your website
- Develop your Christian podcast idea

This brings me around to Mark 5:20. . . you may be wondering why I picked that verse for the name of my publishing imprint.

In Mark 5 (also Matthew 8 and Luke 8), we read of Jesus crossing over the Sea Galilee and casting demons out of a man. The man lived a miserable, tortured life. Mark tells us three times that the man lived among the tombs (vv. 2,3,5), crying out and cutting himself at all hours of the day and night. Then, in a moment with the Savior, he was forever changed. He who was naked and snarling with demonic control now sat **"clothed and in his right mind"** (v. 15). The man then begged Jesus to go with Him. However, Jesus instead told him, **"Go home to your own people. . . and tell them how much the Lord has done for you, and what mercy He has shown you"** (Mark 5:19).

And then, there in Mark 5:20, Mark tells us, **"So the man went away and began to proclaim throughout the Decapolis how much Jesus had done for him. And everyone was amazed."**

All of us who have been born again by the Spirit of God have been healed of something. All of us have been saved from our sins—I know I have! As a result, out of a heart of great gratitude, I want to use the rest of my life to tell others about Jesus, just like the man in Mark 5:20. I want to encourage and inspire believers like you to be like him, too.

A publisher friend of mine, Rick, pointed out to me that Jesus told the man to go and tell others what **"the Lord"** (God) did for him, and what did the man do? He went and proclaimed, **"all that *Jesus* had done for him"** (emphasis added). In other words, the man understood that Jesus was God. (Brilliant observation, Rick!)

It would certainly bolster my case if I could offer you a list of "Twenty-Five Famous Christians Saved by Gospel Tracts or Books," but I can't. To my knowledge, no such list exists on this side of heaven. For one thing, the Lord often uses several means to open the eyes of an unbeliever and bring about conversion. One person scatters seeds, another waters, and another reaps (John 4:37; 1 Cor. 3:3-9). A gospel tract, for example, might be a man's first exposure to the biblical gospel, or God might use it as the last step in breaking him and bringing him to Himself. Remember Jesus' words we considered earlier, **"The wind blows where it wishes. You hear its sound, but you do not know where it comes from or where it is going. So it is with everyone born of the Spirit"** (John 3:8). I once heard a story of someone who left scraps of paper with Bible verses written on them for someone to find. One verse. God's Word does not come back void, so why not (Isa. 55:11)?

God can use scraps of verses, gospel tracts, and all kinds of means in the process of saving people. But whom He saves, when He saves them, and what they go on to do for Him and His Kingdom are known only to God. Also, as someone said, when we lack the means to do a thing for the Lord, He counts the desire to do it as though it were the thing done. That's why you and I need to be content to do what we can and leave the results up to the Lord. It is our job to be faithful to what He's called us to do, which is primarily to love the Lord above all else, love others, and advance the Kingdom through making disciples. The Spirit equips and guides us, and He prepares hearts for the seed of the gospel to be sown. And He waters the seed and causes it to bring forth fruit in its time. All of it is God doing the work and producing the results. You and I are just privileged to take part, like the man in Mark 5:20.

Do you enjoy writing or getting your message out? I assume you do since you are reading this book. I enjoy writing because I enjoy people. I also love ideas and I love the Lord. Writing gives me an outlet to engage in all three dimensions, simultaneously. In my own time, I can engage people with gospel-influenced ideas that glorify

God, and do it relatively affordably, and from anywhere. And I never know whom I am going to "meet" because I never know where the Lord will take my work or who is going to end up reading it. It's exciting. And it's exciting because it's *gospel-exciting*. Gospel work can certainly have its difficult moments, but on the whole it is joyous work. To paraphrase Psalm 84:10, "Better is one day in gospel work than thousands being as rich as Warren Buffet; I would rather take the lowest job with Jesus than the highest job without Him!" I don't know how the Lord may use my small attempts to bring Him glory, but I know that when I try, it delights Him and it excites me.

Being a digital missionary can be a joy. It is a delightful adventure. Yes, it can be lonely and may not seem very adventurous or successful. Case in point: I struggled for two or three days to find the right words to say what I wanted to say in this chapter. Writing can feel that way much of the time. But what a thrill when someone tells me she gave my evangelistic book to a friend or family member to read! What a joy to my soul, what a privilege, that the Lord would use my words in whatever work He is doing in that person's life. That's the kind of impact you, too, can have when you write and publish for Christ.

The Power to Save Even One

Maybe you are not a natural writer. That's okay. Let me let you in on a little secret: When I was a baby, I couldn't even write my own name. I am joking, of course, but you get my point. Even the best writers had to work at it. Besides, you may be a better writer than you give yourself credit for. Many people don't realize that they have been writing emails and business communications for years. Others forget they have been gifted storytellers their whole lives. If that is you, go ahead and audio record your ideas, your experiences, and your story. That audio can be transcribed into a written book or retooled into an audio book.

Are you a pastor? Take a sermon series God used in a special way and publish it so your church members can have a way to share that series with others. You could give copies away as gifts to Sunday-morning visitors. You could leave a copy for those you visit who are homebound or in the hospital.

Are you a prison chaplain or a police officer? Publish a book of stories of how you've seen God save sinners from drugs, alcohol, anger, and violence (leaving out any potentially identifying details, of course).

God can use your book to give hope and share the light of Christ with someone who desperately needs it. It does not need to be a long book. A book of roughly 10,000 words sounds like a lot, but it really isn't. You've read more words than that already in this book. A small book that can be read or listened to in less than an hour can make a lasting impression.

If you had the chance to spend an hour sharing something gospel-related with the barista you see all the time at Starbucks, what would you say? Write it down, publish it, and give it to him or her. Imagine handing that person a copy of your book and being able to say, "Thanks so much for all you do. I wrote this book, and you were one of the people on my heart as I prayed and wrote it."

What advice could you give to the youth group kids

who are about to graduate high school? How can you point them to the Lord and encourage them to walk with Him all their adult lives? What advice can you give them from the Scriptures and life about money management, decision-making, and all the important adult things they will need to know? Write it down and publish it, and you will have a gospel tool you can give out year after year!

How might the Lord use a gospel-centered book published for your ministry organization? What life-changing stories can you share as a life-preserver to throw to those in need of rescue?

I know I may have repeated myself here and there, but I did so for a reason. I wanted to draw your eyes up to the horizon, as it were, to see the fields white for harvest. Your book could be something the Lord uses in the life of even one person to save him or her. It is tempting to be unimpressed by that and shrug. "That is only one person though!" We grumble and complain about "only one person" because *we* have forgotten the value of one human soul. But the Lord hasn't! Imagine if God used your book to help save one sinner from an eternity in the torments of hell. Praise the Lord! That is the power to save that comes with publishing for Christ.

This chapter would not be complete without a look into the far-off future. Imagine the joy you will have when you get to heaven and discover people whom God saved through *your* book—people you never knew in this life; people who maybe did not even speak the same language; or maybe people far into the future from today, who get saved by reading something you wrote one hundred years before they were even born. One day, you may be up in glory while your words live on down here, continuing your labors for the kingdom in your place.

What a privilege! Imagine the hugs and the *thank yous*. Then you both turn to the Lord and thank *Him* because it was all *His* great doing in the first place!

Lastly, imagine, as I do, the day you can walk up to the man of Mark 5:20. You can tell him how his ministry of proclaiming Jesus lived on for thousands of years and touched millions of lives. And you can tell him how much his story inspired you to go to *your* Decapolis and tell the people there what the Lord did for you.

I know I keep using the word but, truly, what a privilege it is that we get to be part of all of this!

5

The Power
to Influence

Think back. Who were some people who have influenced you? And, more to our topic, what authors and their writings have most influenced you in your walk with the Lord? Influence is that sway others can have over our attitudes and behaviors, whether we know it or not. Oftentimes, there is just something about their personality that inspires us to want to be like them or follow their example.

When I was growing up, my parents were not believers, but they influenced me to be kind and treat everybody the same, no matter their color, creed, or whether they were the big boss or security guard in the lobby. Both of my parents could chat it up with anybody. Given enough time, nobody was a stranger. They taught me, influenced me, to be the same way.

Fast forward a few years. I'm a young man in my early twenties working my first real job at a software company. Every day before I left work, I would mix it up with the old man who worked at our security desk in the lobby. Bob was a great guy, always full of stories! Sometimes I would watch in amazement and chuckle to myself when someone would walk out for the night and Bob would wish him good night and he would only grunt or ignore the lowly security guard. Because I got to know Bob, I knew something about him others didn't. Bob wasn't just some old guy supplementing his Social Security by working a lowly security desk. Bob was a retired Secret Service agent who had protected several presidents, and he had shown me the photos to prove it!

Okay, I'll admit it; maybe that is not the best example of influence, but you have to admit, it is a great story! Then again, I would never have known that about Bob if I had not been influenced by my parents to be kind and respectful to people.

One thing is certainly true though: All of us are influenced by others. Sometimes people let themselves be swayed for good, and sometimes for evil. Who has influenced you? And perhaps more importantly, who are you influencing?

One of the best-selling business books of all time is Dale Carnegie's *How to Win Friends and Influence People*. Published in 1936, it was one of the earliest self-help books on the market, has been translated into dozens of languages, and has sold over thirty million copies worldwide. It's nearly one hundred years old and still sells a quarter of a million copies annually. That's a lot of influence!

I wonder what Mr. Carnegie would think of influence today? The world of social media loves to prop up its "influencers," those who promote themselves and their channels, often for their own glory. Recently, I saw a documentary interviewing ordinary Russians who post photos of themselves walking or standing along the narrow ledges of Moscow skyscrapers or posing artfully atop some high bridge or antenna. They will risk a split-second mistake that could plunge them to their deaths for a bit of online fame and glory. They chase after glory, but it's a glory that will fade.

We who are born again by the Spirit eschew such vanity—not because we are better than they are, but because we were dead but have been made alive in Christ (Eph. 2:1-7). For a Christian to seek to become an "influencer" is an oxymoron. That person has forgotten who they truly are and where they came from:

> Brothers, consider the time of your calling: Not many of you were wise by human standards; not many were powerful; not many were of noble birth. But God chose the foolish things of the world to shame the wise; God chose the weak things of the world to shame the strong. He chose the lowly and despised things of the world, and the things that are not, to nullify the things that are, so that no one may boast in His presence. (1 Cor. 1:26-28)

The NIV helps us think about this by translating "**not many were powerful**" as "**not many were influential.**" The world doesn't see us as influencers. It sees us as "**foolish. . . weak. . . lowly and despised. . .**" Things that "**are not.**" Nobodies! How foolish then, that a redeemed-by-grace nobody would seek to shrewdly jockey his or her way to a position of influence in the world or in the Church. Yet we see it all the time.

A true Christian, and truly Christian writing, longs for only one Person to get the glory: the Lord Jesus. He deserves all of it. And the power of publishing for Christ gives exactly that: The power to influence others to seek eternal life that is only found in Him.

The Power of Influence

Let me share a personal story about an "influencer" who was influencing others long before social media. Back when I was a teenager in the mid-late 1980s, maybe sixteen or seventeen, things were not great at home. My parents were separated and, like any kid at that age, I wasn't taking it well. Neither were Christians, but by then I had started attending the Calvary Chapel in my town. Because the church had no building of its own yet, they rented an upstairs room at another church for their midweek Bible studies.

Each week after the Bible study was over, "Frank" would call out my name with great fanfare. "AAAAAAAA-Anthony!" he'd say, mimicking the Italian mother from the old Prince Spaghetti commercial that was popular on television when I was growing up.

Frank knew about my broken home and my ongoing struggles navigating my parents' separation. That's why every week, without fail, Frank took time to pull me aside and check in with me. He was a huge encouragement to me because he asked me questions and he listened. Frank cared. Really cared. And, without fail, Frank ended our five or ten minutes together by praying for me. To know that someone loved me, heard me, and earnestly prayed for the Lord to help and guide me gave me hope.

So, just how influential for Christ was Frank? Well, that was nearly forty years ago, and I am still telling people about him.

Frank influenced me in another way, too. To this day I try to follow his example. I look for others to meet and, if necessary, to pray right there with them, just like Frank did for me.

He'll never know in this life how much those times meant or how they helped shape me to become who I am today. I love that guy and I can't wait for our reunion in heaven, when I hear a voice over my shoulder call out *AAAAAAAAAnthonyyyy!*

Let me tell you a few intertwined stories of the power to influence. Before writing this chapter, I had never heard of Church of England minister Dr. Claudius Buchanan, and I am willing to guess you haven't, either. But if I said the name Adoniram Judson, you would probably know of that legendary missionary to Burma (now Myanmar). We'll begin with these two men.

While Dr. Buchanan's name may have slipped quietly into history, the fruits of his publishing labors live on—in large part because of a sermon he gave which was transcribed and published. You see, while still a student, as a young man Adoniram Judson read that sermon and was stirred by Dr. Buchanan's printed message. Because of that sermon, Judson committed himself to go abroad as a missionary. The rest, as they say, is history.

Buchanan's sermon got published, which influenced Judson. Incidentally, both men were probably themselves inspired by William Carey's published treatise on the need for global missions, *An Enquiry into the Obligation of Christians. . .* which God used as the catalyst of the modern missionary era and is itself another example of the power of publishing to inspire others to action.

Eventually, Judson was financially supported on the mission field through the domestic influence of his friend, Luther Rice. (To say that Rice worked "tirelessly" to rally Baptists together to support the work of missions is not a cliché; in fact, it's probably an understatement!) We'll learn more about Rice a little later.

Speaking of influence, Rice was influenced as teenager by the writings of Richard Baxter, and later his heart was stirred for missions by the published newsletters of the missionary societies in Britain of the day, who sent their updates to America.

The fruit of all these men resulted the salvation of untold numbers of souls and many churches being planted. Judson, a gifted linguist, also translated the Scriptures into the Burmese language. These men have inspired others to the mission field over the last 150 years, even down to today. That is the power of publishing for Christ, and its power to influence. You and I may not be a Buchanan, Carey, or Judson, but with that kind of compounding interest return, it is easy to see why publishing for Christ is well worth the investment.

As I was writing this chapter, I found this quotation by Erroll Hulse in his biography of Adoniram Judson, which further presses the point we are now considering. Consider these powerful words:

Also there to inspire Judson was the biography of David Brainerd (1718-1747) who devoted himself entirely to reach the unreached Indians. He laboured intensely among the Indians for just three years and was the instrument of a powerful spiritual revival. He died at the early age of 29 in the home of Jonathan Edwards (1704-1758) the famous pastor and theologian who used Brainerd's diaries to write his biography. *Historians regard this account of Brainerd's life and labours as having a greater influence to inspire missionary effort than any other book.*"[8]

David Brainerd died without ever knowing the incomprehensible influence his words would have in inspiring men and women to go to the mission field. What a gift Edwards gave the world when he gave us Brainerd's journals!

One of my spiritual heroes is a man I mentioned earlier who has been almost entirely forgotten, Luther Rice. If you have ever read a biography of Adoniram Judson, you will remember the name Luther Rice. As young men, Judson and Rice sailed to India to meet up with the man we now know as "the father of modern missions," William Carey. Because of sickness, Rice could not stay abroad and so he returned home. He may have left the mission field, but the need to reach world's lost souls with the Good News of the Savior never left his heart. He came home and committed the rest of his life to raising support for his friend, Judson, and Baptist missionary efforts. In terms of influence, Luther Rice was a force of nature.

8   *Adoniram Judson and the Missionary Call*. Errol Hulse. Chapel Library. Pensacola, Florida. 1996, page 12, emphasis added.

To put his efforts in perspective, before Luther Rice's time, the Baptist churches in the young nation were independent in both missions endeavors and funding. But it was Rice who traveled thousands of miles on horseback and buggy, up and down the eastern seaboard many times over, to influence and rally these churches to form a coalition to finance and support Judson and other missionary endeavors. John Wesley before him was known for the great distances he would travel in England on horseback. Luther Rice broke Wesley's record for a single day's horseback travel by traveling ninety-three miles in a single day (compared to Wesley's record ninety miles). Rice worked to form what we know of today as the International Mission Board of the Southern Baptist Convention. If it wasn't for Luther Rice and his willingness to crisscross the rugged landscape of nineteenth-century America at any personal cost, Adoniram Judson almost certainly would not have been able to remain in Burma.

Rice's story of influence does not end there, either. Rice was passionate about education. Through his efforts, he also influenced the Baptists to fund educational efforts. A national Baptist college was established on the outskirts of Washington, DC, called Columbian College. Today, although it is no longer a Baptist college, and no longer even Christian, most people know the school as the renowned George Washington University.

Rice wasn't a writer. He wasn't widely published. He kept a detailed diary, which was a popular thing to do in those days, and this has been preserved, but even that is not widely published. He preached most everywhere he traveled, but to my knowledge none of his sermons was printed. So why mention him in a book on publishing? For two reasons.

First, I mention him because he has become a spiritual hero to me. Rice faced a crushing defeat when he had to come off the mission field, for it was his life's dream. He even broke off his engagement to the love of his life when she was unwilling to join him. His story reminds us to never take defeat sitting down. Get up. Look for something else to do instead. Rice was a man of boundless energy and influence. We need more men like him. And so, in my own small way, I am privileged to honor him and his legacy, sharing his influence on me so that he can, in turn, influence you.

Second, I mention him because this is a chapter on the power of influence, and Rice's life was spent influencing others to unite and to mobilize for the great cause of Christ in the sphere of global missions. What a testimony to the power of being a *real* "influencer"!

Are You in the Saddle?

I will never be a Luther Rice. I will never travel thousands of miles up and down the nation to influence people. You probably won't get that kind of opportunity either. That's okay. We can't all be Luther Rices. But Rice's life does challenge us, doesn't it? We may not cover the miles that Luther Rice did in his day, but are we "in the saddle" at all? Are we even trying?

We probably won't be Brainerds either, but publishing gives us the power to influence people we may never meet on this side of eternity.

Are you maximizing what influence God *has* given you?

Are you influencing those whom God has put in your path, helping them *Know, Grow,* and *Go?* Get involved in publishing. Pray and ask the Lord how you may glorify Him and influence others for Christ via publishing.

If I can share another personal testimony with you: Because of those who were obedient to the call to publish for Christ, I have been comforted in seasons of midnight despair, rebuked when clinging to private sin, and encouraged, helped, and mentored by some of the best Christian minds outside of sacred Scripture. Godly men who lived centuries ago have graciously given me counsel in dark, lonely hours when it would be impossible to meet with a pastor or call a friend. The list of writers I have to thank in heaven is long. That's the kind of influence writing and publishing have. Who might draw midnight hope from your words?

Two quotations from the Puritan Thomas Brooks illustrate this point: "Books may preach when the author cannot, when the author may not, when the author dares not, yes, and which is more, when the author is not."[9] And, "What is written is permanent, and spreads itself further by far—for time, place, and people—than the voice can reach."[10]

Inherent in this power to influence is the power to multiply. You share some truth which the Lord showed you from the Scriptures or you read from someone else, and you pass it on. Your readers are now informed and they, in turn, may one day pass that truth on to someone else, and so on. . .

My training is in biblical counseling. I help others navigate the problems of life by opening the Scriptures with

9   https://www.gracegems.org/Brooks/heaven_on_earth8.htm
10   Thomas Brooks, *The Mute Christian Under the Smarting Rod*

them to see what God has said about their problem and what counsel He gives about it. I hope to write about particular issues so that I can help more people than I could in the counseling room. Consider the math: A small book that takes two hours to read or listen to, if read by even a hundred people, would take me 200 hours in the counseling room to communicate. Instead, I can "meet" with them anytime that is convenient for them through a book. And it is the comforted-to-pass-it-on principle Paul writes of in 2 Corinthians 1. It's the power to multiply.

Not From the East or From the West

Earlier, we reflected on the folly of those who chase after being a social media "influencer." I want to return to that topic for a moment to add a word of related caution: Beware of seeking a platform yourself. Beware of the temptation to promote *Self*. This never looks good. I have seen authors over the years who use their social media to include quote graphics in which they are quoting none other than *themselves!* Some go so far as to include a little brand logo that is a kind of cartoon likeness of themselves. "Cringe" is a popular word these days, and that's exactly what I do every time I see this trend pop up in my social media feed. Some of these authors likely have other people running their social media for them, but still. . .

Can you imagine if social media existed in the first century? Would John the Baptist be quoting himself, the great herald of the Promised One? Would the Lord Jesus promote Himself like some of His followers promote themselves? Can you imagine the apostle Paul posting a quote graphic of something he said, like

FOR IT IS BY GRACE YOU ARE SAVED, THROUGH
FAITH, AND NOT OF YOURSELVES.
@THEAPOSTLEPAUL
#FOLLOWMEASIFOLLOWCHRIST

Absurd, right?

It is true, sometimes the Lord does raise up someone and gives that person a platform and a voice. But that is different. That is the Lord's doing.

We see this, for example, in the opening chapters of 1 Samuel. Those first few chapters are both thrilling and terrifying. On the one hand, we see how the Lord graciously takes away Hannah's sorrow and shame and answers her prayers for a child who would become the prophet, Samuel. In contrast, we also read about the evils of Eli's priestly sons, Hophni and Phineas. In short order, God proclaims imminent judgment and death on Eli's worthless sons and how the entire family line would forever be under God's judgment. At the same time, the Lord elevates Samuel to replace them, **"And Samuel grew, and the LORD was with him, and He let none of Samuel's words fall to the ground. So all Israel from Dan to Beersheba knew that Samuel was confirmed as a prophet of the LORD,"** (1 Sam. 3:19-20).

The Lord raises up whom He will raise up. Look also at the words of the psalmist:

For exaltation comes neither from east nor west,
nor out of the desert,
but it is God who judges;
He brings down one and exalts another.
(Ps. 75:6-7)

Forget building a platform! Deny yourself, take up your cross, and follow Christ. Embrace John the Baptist's desire in John 3:30 as your own, **"He must increase; I must decrease."** And Paul's, **"For we do not proclaim ourselves, but Jesus Christ as Lord, and ourselves as your servants for Jesus' sake,"** (2 Cor. 4:5). And, above all, consider the very example of our Lord, who **"made himself nothing"** (Phil. 2:7 KJV). Since the sovereign God of the universe, in the Second Person of the Trinity, came to earth and made Himself nothing, doesn't it seem ludicrous that we would try to make ourselves something?

George Whitefield said, "Let the name of George Whitfield perish so long as Christ is exalted!" Adoniram Judson, like Whitefield before him, also ended up becoming famous while he was still alive but he never once sought it. He downplayed his fame at every opportunity. One of his rules for himself that we would do well to adopt ourselves is, "Undertake nothing from motives of ambition, or love of fame." At the risk of pressing the point, consider these words from Charles Spurgeon: "Be content to be nothing, for that is what you are." Scripture says that the Lord remembers that we are dust (Ps. 103:14). We are the ones who constantly forget that.

It's been my own experience to observe that those Christians who chase after building a platform and making a name for themselves either experience frustration when the Lord does not bless their efforts or, worse, they get what they want, and it ruins them. If the Lord wants you or me to have a greater, wider influence, He will raise us up in His time and in His way.

Of all those who influence us, may we be influenced

by God Himself most of all. It is dangerously easy to write a Christian book without being in close fellowship with Christ. Judging some of the things that get published in the name of Christ, it happens all the time—just like every Sunday there are thousands of ministerial professionals in pulpits who do not know God. These people are ignorant of the awful truth that His wrath abides on them. On the Great Day, there will be scores and scores of authors who will cry out before their Judge, "Lord, Lord, did we not write books about You?" And He will "tell them plainly, 'I never knew you; depart from Me, you workers of lawlessness!'" (Matt. 7:23).

Christians who write, blog, or podcast are busy people. They are writing new material, researching for future projects, developing marketing, working multiple social media channels, updating their website, and forever trying to figure out and appease the latest SEO standards. But we must never be so busy that we don't take time to pray and be in the Scriptures for the benefit and sanctification of our own souls.

Remember Mary and Martha? Preparing a meal for the Lord was nice, but Mary wisely knew when to sit and listen at the feet of the Lord. Martin Luther is famously reported to have said, "I have so much to do that I shall spend the first three hours in prayer." Whether he did or not is inconclusive, but the point remains: How can we expect the Lord to bless our efforts if we don't make Him our number one priority every single day? **"Behold, obedience is better than sacrifice,"** the Lord tells us (1 Sam. 15:22). Better to love the Lord with all our heart, soul, mind, and strength than to be so busy in our quest to do something for the Lord that we neglect Him entirely.

We must not be Laodiceans. We mustn't lose our first love. Jesus said, **"I am the vine and you are the branches. The one who remains in Me, and I in him, will bear much fruit. For apart from Me you can do nothing."** (John 15:5). In our desire to do something for God, we must not go forward without Him, or strive to make a name for ourselves, but rather make it all about that Name Above All Names.

6

The Power
to Reach

Who are you praying for, that they would come to know the Lord? What about your friend at the gym? What about the shift lead at the local coffee shop you've been spending a lot of time at, who knows your name, that you like dark roast coffee, and that chocolate chip cookies are your Kryptonite? (Wait, that's not you, that's me.) This chapter is about you being able to do something almost eight-billion other people cannot do: You can reach that person with the gospel.

What if you had a tool—no, better—a *gift*? That's right. What if you had a personalized gift, written by you, for everyone you have the power to reach? Imagine being able to hand someone a book with your name on it to make that connection a little more personal, that gift a little more intriguing?

You don't have to write the greatest book ever (the Lord already did that, anyway). You just have to—and you *get to*—write something that points people to Jesus.

The man Jesus healed in Mark 5:20 went back to the

Decapolis region and spread the word about the Lord who healed and saved him. That's the power of reach and spark of connection you can have, too.

Where is your Decapolis? Where is your Judea? Samaria? What if you really could help take the gospel to the ends of the earth?

You *can* write a book to highlight your ministry, or as a tool for personal evangelism, or for whatever gospel reason, if that's what you have a desire to do. And like I said at the beginning, if you want to write a how-to book, novel, memoir, or whatever to the glory of God, do it. If you have the slightest inkling to write and publish, you should, *and you can.*

In the previous chapter I talked about the power of influence of men and women I have read over the years. I have been blessed by the writings of many men and women who long ago passed into glory, but their published words live on. They not only influenced believers of their day, but their reach extends across time. Some have become recognized and are well known. Others, less so. And still others are completely unknown to us, but their words have been digitally preserved in a file available for download from some Christian corner of the Internet. In every case, those men and women wrote something for the cause of Christ, and the Lord has used it in my life, I am guessing in your life, and in the lives of many others.

Answering the call to be a digital missionary offers you potential to reach people. Write and publish for Christ and you may reach into the lives of those whom you would never otherwise have had the opportunity. By God's providence, your "words fitly spoken" may reach them at the exact right season for them. You may never know about it this side of eternity, but it happens for writers every day.

The Book is the Missionary

What would you say if I told you that, for roughly the same cost as a one- or two-week, short-term mission trip, you might reach generations for Christ?

When we talk about the power to reach, who are we reaching? The unreached. Who are the "unreached"? That depends. If you are a ministry leader, any potential ministry partner who hasn't heard of the work your ministry is doing is your "unreached." If you are a business owner, anyone who would buy your product or service is your "unreached." For me writing this book, any Christian who has a desire to write and publish something specifically gospel-related is my "unreached." And, most important of all, anyone you want to tell about Jesus is your "unreached." Your unreached don't have to live half a world away, they can be as near as a lost loved one, the neighbor who walks her dog past your house every day, the nurse at the doctor's office, or your child's teacher.

In missionary endeavors, we seek to reach the lost—to reach the unreached. Publishing something specifically for the purpose of making disciples for Christ is taking part in the Great Commission. Your book may circulate in your Judea. It may reach your Samaria. Or the Lord may give an opportunity for your published words to travel to distant lands on your behalf, making disciples and teaching them all that Jesus commanded (Matt. 28:19-20). You may not be able to *Go*, but your book can. The book is the missionary.

I can vouch for what I am suggesting. Months after I returned from my short-term mission trip to the African country of Burundi, I got a WhatsApp message from a brother there. He had given the French-language copy of my evangelistic book *Jesus Changed Everything* to his nephew to read, who was visiting from France. Isn't that amazing! There was a young man from France whom I would never have met, reading my book giving the gospel in a language I can't speak or write, in a country I only visited for four days! Praise the Lord!

In their book *Introduction to Global Missions*, Pratt, Sills, and Walters write that "Missionaries are limited in the number of people they can evangelize, churches they can plant, disciples they can train, and pastors they can teach" (199).[11] But think about it: For every culture that is a literate culture, a quality Christian book can be a tireless in-country missionary helper. Apart from the Bible itself, the greatest tool for reaching men and women for Christ will always be other men and women, but in their physical absence, a quality Christian book can be helpful stand-in.

Speaking of quality, as Christians, whatever we do should have with it an excellence, and this includes what we write and publish. It is better to not publish at all than to put out a rushed-to-print, lazy book of poor quality. Frankly, the Christian world has far too much of those already. Aim high and give it your best.

Writing and publishing gospel-centered, Christ-honoring literature is a fantastic way to do one's part to fulfill the Great Commission. We have already considered how,

---

11   Zane Pratt, M. David Sills, Jeff K. Walters. *Introduction to Global Missions*. B&H Publishing Group, Nashville, 2014, page 199.

as far as technology and communication go, there has never been a better time in history to seize the opportunity of writing and publishing for Christ. But consider, too, that more and more of the world is learning and speaking English, so more and more people worldwide can read and benefit from English-language books. And we have only scratched the surface of using artificial intelligence (AI) to aid in translation efforts.

The digital world is getting smaller, too. Every day, more remote parts of the world are getting access to the Internet that did not have it before. In 2019, I traveled to Uganda. I was amazed to see people out in the villages still living in rudimentary mud-brick houses with no electricity or running water, but they had a small solar panel on the roof with a USB charger on the end so they could charge their cell phones! In parts of the world where Christianity is restricted, some Christians can have copies of the Scriptures and other literature on USB drives or tucked away in hidden folders on their phones.

Think back fifty years ago. The power to reach was nothing like it is today. How likely would someone on the other side of the world have been able to get a copy of your indie-published book? It would've been nearly impossible, or highly unlikely at best. But today, that's all changed.

Now let's look ahead and think about twenty years into the future.

We can't even imagine what technology will exist. Twenty years ago, in 2004, the world was still three years away from a device that changed how we communicate: the iPhone. Sure, cell phones were not new; they had been around for a while. But after Apple introduced the iPhone in 2007, it literally changed the world. And, although there were others before it, that same year Amazon released the first Kindle E-reader. In twenty years, those revolutionary devices may be on the same retro tech heap as the VCRs and fax machines that came before them.

We also often overlook the power of reach, the lifespan, that a book can have.

As I write this, the automatic desktop wallpaper on my computer updated with a new background. It's a beautiful winter scene of a tree-lined path in Bavaria, right after sunrise. The walking path is flanked on either side by stately rows of mature birch trees. Each branch is covered in ice, making the unbroken row of trees appear to be covered in a full winter "bloom" of ice and snow. In the background, the flat walking path leads the eyes to meet snow-capped mountains. The stunning winter beauty evokes words like "enchanted" and "magical," even though I know it is the Lord's glory on display. I am distracted from writing, my mind transporting me there to walk the path. I can hear the crunch of the morning ice under my feet and imagine the brilliant early-morning orange sunlight reflecting in the ice on the trees.

As I stare at the photograph, another thought comes to mind: The meticulous care that went into planting those trees by someone long ago. A quick Google search tells me it wasn't as long ago as it looks. Fully mature birch trees can apparently reach some forty feet in height in just twenty years. Okay, so not the eighty or a hundred years I was thinking, but the lesson is there for us still. Are you writing only to sell a few books in the next few months or year, or are you planting birch trees for people to walk under decades from now?

It's easy to get caught up in the world's pace of things. Who wouldn't want instant results? I have worked in Information Technology for three decades. Even the slow computers that existed when I got into the field were light-years ahead of their predecessors. And now the smart phones that you and I hold in our hands are light-years ahead of those early home computers. That's the age we live in—fast and faster, all the time.

My point is this: I am so far from having a natural, slow agrarian mindset that I can't imagine waiting three years or more for a fruit tree to mature. I would not normally think to plant a birch tree today, in my early fifties, so that I can enjoy its shade when I am in my mid-seventies. But that is exactly the mindset we need to have, both in life and in waiting for fruit from what we write and publish for Christ.

As I write this, it's the end of 2023. I stop for a minute to reread what I wrote, and I am challenged by my own words. *Lord, if it should please You to allow it, who might read this book in 2043, or beyond? I pray it blesses them and stirs them to know, love, and serve You more, and to write something doctrinally sound to glorify You and benefit Your people.* (And, if you are reading this in 2043, hello and thank you!)

In Zechariah 4:10, we are taught not to despise small beginnings when the Lord is in the work. In the New Testament, Jesus taught us that even the simple act of giving a cup of cold water to a brother or sister in Christ would be rewarded (Matt. 10:42; Mark 9:41). Who can tell what the Lord might do from your small beginning?

Do you know why I started to write and publish? I was working from home, out of the basement in our cold Louisville, Kentucky, basement, doing IT project management. I hardly got out to see and interact with other people. Years before, I had started a blog. After a while, I had enough old blog posts that I wanted to compile the best of them into a book, just to say that I wrote one book in my life. God wired me to want to write a book, and, by His grace, I did!

That was my first book, originally titled *Pleasant Places: Short Essays on the Christian Life,* published in 2014.[12]

That was it. Goal achieved. I did not write another book for seven years. I thought about it, but I never disciplined myself to do it again.

Amazingly, in 2021, I found myself in the same situation: I was working from home and not getting much opportunity to be around people. (Thankfully, by then I was out of the basement and out of Louisville, and in the warmer climate of South Carolina.) I missed talking to people about Jesus in the course of life. Then I read a book on evangelism by a man (I forget who) who challenged his readers: Handing out other people's Christian literature is great, but if you want to make a personal connection with someone, hand them something with your name on the cover. That was the spark that fired up the engine again.

Challenge accepted.

In a matter of weeks or maybe months, I cranked out *Jesus Changed Everything: He Changed History, He Can Change Your Story.* It's an easy-to-read book that has one goal: Give someone the gospel. It's written as if I am privileged to meet the reader over coffee. I have an hour or

12   Seven years later, in 2021, I republished it and slightly changed the subtitle.

so to share the gospel. As I was writing it, I thought, *What would I say if I were dying, if these were my last words? What would I say if I had an hour with this person to talk about the Lord and would never see him again?* Since publication, I can tell you that that other author was right: Having my name on the cover made a difference to some people. Having *your* name on the cover of your book will make a difference to someone, too.

In 2023 I had the privilege of being invited to Burundi and Uganda, along with another brother. He was conducting another lesson in his ongoing marriage seminar with believers there, and I was asked to speak on the topic of "The minister and his marriage." By now my thinking had radically shifted! I went from thinking how difficult it was in 2014 to realizing how absolutely doable it is, and how worthwhile the end result would be.

So, as I got to thinking about my topic, I decided that instead of simply bringing stapled handouts to share, I would write a book and hand that out instead, plus it made an attractive *thank you* gift for the opportunity.

For that book, the old writing engine cranked up even faster! I wrote the first draft in only a week. It helped that I only had about six weeks to go from idea to finished product if I was going to have it ready to take with me. The great Duke Ellington's words of wisdom rang true: *I don't need time. I need a deadline.* I agree. I always work best when the countdown clock is ticking. This time, that tight deadline produced *LOVE, LEAD, SERVE: The Christian Man's Call to Lead His Family and His Church.*

And you know what I was doing for that book, too? You guess it—the same thing I was doing for the first ones: IT project management, working from the confines of my home office. And again, I was fueled by the same desire: to reach the world for Jesus from this spare bedroom home office. This time He was kind enough to let me reach all the way to Africa!

And now I am amazed at God's goodness once again; here I am, still holed up in my home office, still doing IT project management, and yet cranking out an astonishing *fifth* book in my spare time! I am just a guy from New Jersey who barely graduated high school! Only the kindness of our loving God could do all this!

And if I can do it, so can you.

That sense of wanting to get out and do more but the Lord leaving me here in the home office is another reason the man in Mark 5:20 inspires me. It wasn't the Lord's will that he join Him in His travels, but the Lord had him go back and work the harvest in other fields. The Lord providentially hindered me from going to be a missionary, so I am cranking out books to tell others about Him, right from my own home, because that is something I can do for Him.

What about you? Where does the Lord have you? Don't make the same mistake I did for so long (and really, it was sin)—Don't grumble to the Lord that you would be so much better used over there than where He has you here. Be faithful here, where you are, because "here" is where God has ordained you to be. Do what you can where you are. Enjoy your humble seat at His banquet table—and praise Him that you are at His table at all! And if He is pleased to call you to come and sit in a place of greater honor at that table, giving you a platform to speak from, fine, but if not, also fine (Luke 14:10). Write and publish where you are, and trust the Lord to perhaps carry your words to your neighbors, to Africa, or beyond!

You Never Know

Cast your bread upon the waters,
>for you will find it after many days.
Give a portion to seven, or even to eight,
>for you know not what disaster may happen
on earth.
If the clouds are full of rain,
>they empty themselves on the earth,
and if a tree falls to the south or to the north,
>in the place where the tree falls, there it will
lie.
He who observes the wind will not sow,
>and he who regards the clouds will not reap.

As you do not know the way the spirit comes to the bones in the womb of a woman with child, so you do not know the work of God who makes everything.
In the morning sow your seed, and at evening withhold not your hand, for you do not know which will prosper, this or that, or whether both alike will be good.
(Eccl. 11:1-6)

I have already told you how I enjoy finding obscure tidbits of Christian writings on the Internet. Permit me to share a few lines from Methodist minister and Professor of New Testament at New College in London, T. Francis Glasson, who in his writing on this passage focuses on the phrase which, in our modern English essentially translates to "you never know" and occurs four times in this passage. Glasson writes:

> We need the spirit of venture, of hope and faith, the conviction that in due season we shall reap if we faint not, even if it is only "after many days" that the full returns appear. We must sow at all times and even in the most unlikely places with a kind of reckless optimism, not waiting for ideal conditions.[13]

In short, Glasson sees it as a message of optimistic encouragement to be industrious, to attempt things, because, well, "you never know"! He goes on to add:

> Without trying to match the four occurrences of the phrase with any exactness, I find in this passage a number of pertinent reminders. (1). You never know what may happen in unlikely places; (2). you never know what may happen at odd times and even in unfavourable seasons; (3). you never know what may emerge 'after many days'; and (4). you never know what God is doing through your service, whether in preaching the Word or teaching the young or in personal testimony and influence. We must sow everywhere, in the unlikeliest places.[14]

13   https://biblicalstudies.org.uk/pdf/eq/1983-1_043.pdf
14   Ibid.

And, lastly, he shares this story:

> I remember taking a journey through a very quiet part of England, a countryside where "nothing important ever happens", away from the busy highways. But on that single journey I passed places associated with Wm. Carey, Wm. Cowper, John Newton and John Bunyan. Think what those four men have contributed to the spiritual life of the whole world. If God has set you in an obscure spot, you never know what may ultimately spring from some life you will touch; and quite apart from that every soul is of infinite value in His sight.[15]

I read Glasson's insights with great encouragement. I have already cited examples from my own life of this "you never know" principle at work. I sit here excited and wondering what "you never know" results may happen if you go on a "digital missions trip" or commit to be a long-term digital missionary and answer the call to publish for Christ.

No chapter about reach would be complete without discussing the apostle Paul. Whether locked up in a dank and miserable Roman dungeon or under a more comfortable but still restricted house arrest, what did he do? Did he languish there, pining and whining to God to get him out so he could do great things for God as a free man? No! He had such determination that even where he was, he was unstoppable. The Roman Empire may have locked him up, but it was powerless to shut him down.

What did he do?

15   Ibid.

He wrote! He published! He dictated his letters, and they were sent around and around on the outside, encouraging all the saints across the known world at that time.

Talk about reach!

It all just goes to show: No matter where you are, you can write and publish to do something and reach someone for the Lord Jesus. You can be a digital missionary. Our published words can travel farther and more cheaply than we can. They can be translated into languages we can't speak to reach people we will never meet. And they will outlive us. A book is a missionary, so publish for Christ and take full advantage of its power to reach.

7

The Power
to Heal

When I say that publishing for Christ has the power to heal, what I am saying is every truly Christian book inevitably comes around to some aspect of the gospel, and the gospel brings healing. So, while your book idea may not be on a heavy-duty life issue such as suffering and loss, in this chapter I want to encourage you to publish it if you believe it would do someone some good. God can use it to encourage the downcast, to lift burdens and to bring hope.

Give the Gift of Hope

You may still be skeptical about what I am saying. I can appreciate that. Let me ask you: Have you ever read a Christian biography? My favorites are missionary biographies, partly because I am naturally interested in missions and different cultures. Biographies of Christians minister to me. I see what great difficulties some saints went through, and how the Lord delivered them time and again. Even martyrs get delivered from their trials when the Lord brings them through that last test and into His arms.

Those stories bring hope because it is easy to see our trials as ominous and looming. Christian biographies help put proper perspective to our problems, reminding us that we typically go through far less than they ever did, and encouraging us that the Lord is with us, too, and will see us through whatever He allows in our lives. In other words, those books have with them an element of healing. And so may yours.

Ever since Satan's deceitful ploy worked in the Garden, this world has been ruined by sin. Sin has corrupted everything and everyone. We suffer the ruinous consequences of our sin or are caught in the crossfire of the sins of others. Just as people enter the Emergency Room for a multitude of reasons, there are countless woes in this fallen world.

This world needs healing.

The lost need healing.

We need healing.

That is why this world needs Christians to publish books that have in them the power to heal. We are the only ones who have the only message which offers true and lasting healing.

Consider Peter's words in Acts 10:

> . . . how God anointed Jesus of Nazareth with the Holy Spirit and with power, and how Jesus went around doing good and healing all who were oppressed by the devil, because God was with Him. (Acts 10:38)

One morning not long ago I was reflecting on this verse. It's a wonderful summary of the Lord Jesus' earthly ministry. I reflected on how the Lord is also our role model; we are to pattern our lives after His blessed example. The Lord has us here so that, in our own small way, we can imitate Him, doing good and bringing healing to the oppressed. It is now our privilege to bring the gospel of peace and hope to the world, to love a stranger, and care for those with wounds (physical and emotional) inflicted upon them while living in this sin-cursed, fallen world.

Which brings us back around to my premise for this chapter: Writing and publishing for Christ has within it the power to heal. When we tell others how the Lord can heal their pain, when we testify to how the Lord healed broken relationships, when we offer wise counsel from His Word to address problems of the heart, we are ministering healing in Jesus' name.

As they read our books, it is our job to carry them on their mats as it were, breaking through the roof, and lowering them to Jesus for forgiveness and healing. We are offering a cup of cold water to the tired and weary. We are coming alongside to be burden-bearers with our readers. The Lord is glorified, and others are helped. What a precious benefit of our efforts to share Christ through the written word. Again, the word "privilege" comes to mind.

Think with me for a moment about this power of the written word to bring healing.

The Lord, as part of His kindness to reveal Himself through the inspired Scriptures, included the Psalms. They were the great worship hymnal of Israel. But they are also solace for the weary, the storm-tossed, and the forsaken. They point us to the Lord who is our Creator and Comforter, our Rock and our Refuge. God alone is man's only hope and our eternally safe haven. Publishing for Christ, we can open the Scriptures and share how God used the Psalms (or any part of His Word) in our lives and share hope and healing with others.

I think of the writings of the Puritans, those stalwarts of the faith. Men like Thomas Watson, Thomas Brooks, Richard Baxter, John Flavel, Samuel Rutherford, Richard Sibbes, and so many others had hearts aglow with pastoral care for the souls of their people and the gifted intellects to put pen to paper to apply Scripture to address their needs.

Another one of my favorite books, and one the Lord used in my life, was a small book by Gardiner Spring, called *The Mission of Sorrow*. Spring was the pastor of his New York City church for over sixty years. His work, though a mere eighty pages long, is a masterpiece about the travails of this life, and a great source of comfort.

There is a mine full of treasures in the writings of men from the late 1800s and early 1900s—men like F.B. Meyer, C.E. Orr, and Vance Havner. They write plainly and share much practical godly wisdom for everyday living, helping readers navigate the ordinary problems of life.

And not to be excluded from the list, plenty of godly women also wrote and published excellent books that offered hope and healing. Elizabeth George, Elisabeth Elliot, Lettie Cowman (she published under her husband's name as Mrs. Charles E. Cowman) have written works which continue to minister to men and women long after these ladies have gone on to their eternal rewards.

I have already mentioned how pastors can transcribe their most helpful sermons into books. Perhaps the most famous example of this as it relates to the power to heal is twentieth-century preacher, Dr. D. Martyn Lloyd-Jones, and his famous book, *Spiritual Depression: Its Causes and Cure*. Iain H. Murray preserved Lloyd-Jones' retelling of they came to be, an experience every preacher can relate to:

> I got up one morning, washed and was still half-dressed when quite suddenly that verse came to me, "Why art thou cast down, O my soul? And why art thou disquieted in me? Hope thou in God. . ." There and then some seven or eight skeletons of sermons came to my mind on the subject of Spiritual Depression. I rushed down to my study to put them on paper and so powerful was the impression that I knew I had to do this series before Ephesians. I am not surprised it was so used. It was a pure gift.[16]

That was 1954. Those twenty-four sermons were soon after transcribed and published. Today, seventy years after they were delivered and forty years after his death, Lloyd-Jones' messages are still in print, still giving hope, and still helping others heal by pointing them to the Lord Jesus Christ.

A generation later, Dr. Jay E. Adams first published his groundbreaking book on pastoral counseling, *Competent to Counsel* in 1971, in opposition to the secular counseling philosophies which had crept into the church and

16   Iain H. Murray, *The Fight of Faith*, Edinburgh, Banner of Truth, 1990, page 259.

the resulting pastoral timidity and reticence to counsel that they had caused. Adams' work sparked the modern biblical counseling movement, arguing that man's ideas about himself and his problems are incomplete and ineffective, and that the Scriptures are our highest and best resource to bring true healing to people and their problems. Adams would go on to write over 150 books, most of which were written to help pastors and lay Christians use the Scriptures to address peoples' questions and problems.

Because of the biblical counseling movement begun by Adams there are, without a doubt, more Christian books available today providing biblical wisdom about issues of the heart than ever before. It has never been easier for someone equipped with sound theology to write and publish a book to help Christians in various trials and point unbelievers to the Great Physician.

In Chapter 3, we looked at Proverbs 13:17b, ". . .a faithful envoy brings healing," and focused on the aspect of being an envoy for Christ. What is the message the envoy brings? A message of healing.

Dr. Anne Dryburgh (annedryburgh.com) has been a trustworthy envoy bringing healing to women in Belgium for nearly thirty years, dedicating most of her life to counseling women who have experienced physical or emotional abuse. She has published four abuse-related books which have helped many women over the years. Her books have also helped raise awareness of abuse and sought to equip churches and Christians to counsel victims with biblical hope and wisdom.

I asked Anne to comment on writing and publishing

for Christ, and the power it has to help bring healing to others. Here is what she wrote:

> Why do I write? I write to in some small way encourage people to know and experience the Lord's gracious help with life's struggles. Sometimes you hear back from people, sharing how they are experiencing the Lord's gracious help. Like this text from a friend who lives in another country: "I met with a friend last night—I told her about your book *The Emotionally Abusive Parent*—She told me the book changed her life. She said she reads it like a devotional. . . I knew she grew up with an abusive dad, but she said it has helped her keep a focus on the gospel when dealing with her mom. She said she loves the book because it is so gospel-focused."[17]

You and I become envoys with words of healing when we apply the balm of Scriptures to the hurting. Through godly counsel, your words offer genuine hope in an otherwise hopeless world, helping others see the goodness of God and pointing them to Him to receive healing from pain, trauma, and grief.

You also become an envoy with words of healing for broken relationships. We have already considered how your words extend the ministry of reconciliation to which you have been called, pointing people to their need to be reconciled with God. But your words also expand your ministry as a peacemaker (Matt. 5:9). You can use the Scriptures to mediate a dispute between parties

17 Personal correspondence. Reprinted with permission.

you may never meet, helping to tear down walls of division, root out bitterness, and replace anger with forgiveness.

And you become an envoy with a message of healing when, like our man in Mark 5:20, you share your own testimony of what the Lord has done to heal you.

The Power of Story

Human beings love stories. We can't get enough of them. Every movie, every novel, every business TED Talk on YouTube is story-driven. We love stories so much that when the Hollywood studios decide to remake an old film, we pay money to be retold the same old story we've known for years!

Of course, we also think of how the Lord Jesus told stories. His parables were always engaging. Even when they were told in rebuke, He captivated His hearers.

And what did Jesus tell our man in Mark 5:20 to do? To go back home to his region and tell people there all that the Lord had done for him.

By publishing your testimony of what God has done in your life, you share how God helped you overcome grief, a job loss, heartache from a wayward son or daughter, fear, uncertainty, and all the other trials and tribulations of life. Your story of God and His goodness can comfort others and give hope to someone who desperately needs it.

People need to know that whatever has happened in their past, whatever they are facing at present, is not unique (1 Cor. 10:13). God has always provided a way of escape, a path to healing, for His children, no matter what they have faced in this world.

You and I are envoys the great hope of salvation in Jesus Christ. The gospel is Good News for this life and for all eternity. It's *the* message to sinners. God's glorious announcement that they can be forgiven, and their punishment taken by the Son of God who loved them and gave Himself up for them (Gal. 2:20), a message that, if acted upon through repentance and faith, brings healing to their guilt-ridden conscience. Ultimately, the great and final work of healing is when the Lord takes us from this world and brings us home to forever be in the arms of our Savior in glory, where there are no tears and no traumas, because sin and death are fully and finally defeated.

We are envoys to carry this wonderful news to those who haven't heard or still refuse to believe it's true.

Given what I said about the number of counseling and heart issues / life-problem books already out there, it is tempting to think *Why bother?* Why should you take the time and effort to write a book that can bring healing when there are already so many others who have, and maybe have said it better, and have a far greater audience than you do?

I ask myself that same basic question with every book I write! Let me give you some encouragement:

It's true, God has gifted His church with many brilliant minds who have decades of pastoral or counseling experience. But not everyone can read what such people have written. Some write for the general reader, but still their book is too academic for their intended audience. For example, I have read worthwhile books on counseling topics that were very helpful, but they were far too long for anyone not accustomed to reading. Some people need something much shorter. Others may need a book addressing a common topic but from an uncommon perspective, like a book about abuse but for men who have been abused by their wives. That is a very specific topic.

Why bother? Because you have a voice and a manner of writing God can use to reach some people that the writings of others cannot reach.

This brings us again back to 2 Corinthians 1. Because the Lord has brought healing and comfort to us, we can pass that word of healing, comfort, and hope to the world. It was Oswald Chambers who said,

> When you are in the dark, listen, and God will give you a very precious message for someone else when you get into the light.[18]

Another point is that if you believe the Lord is nudging you to write a book to offer help and healing, just like with anything else, you need to pray about it, look for the Lord's confirmation, and be obedient to His leading if your circumstances are lining up with green lights and go-aheads.

Maybe God is not calling you to write a book addressing a serious life issue someone needs healing for, but if you have the means, would you consider supporting a missionary like Anne Dryburgh, so she can continue ministering to women and writing books that will live on and bring help and healing long after she's gone? How exciting would it be for you to have a part in the work God is doing through her?

18   https://utmost.org/classic/the-discipline-of-heeding-classic/

This is the privilege you and I share in this endeavor of publishing for Christ: This is the power of healing, and with it comes the duty to ask the Lord, *What is my part?*

8

The Power
to Partner

Tthis chapter was originally going to focus on ministry leaders, those pastors and leaders of para-church ministries looking to grow their ministry audience or donor base. But the more I reflected upon it, the more it occurred to me that the power to partner is so much more than that dynamic. It's not just ministries who need partners. *All of us* need partners. And *all of us* are partners to someone else. The power to partner is about making connections. Sometimes it's us asking others, "Would you help?" and sometimes it's us proactively coming alongside someone else and saying, "I'm excited about what God is doing here. How can I help?"

Pathway to Partnering

Because all of us are partners to someone else, books that tell us what God is doing inform and shape us. We become reminded of the plight of the homeless, the difficulties faced by our brothers and sisters in Christ in hostile lands, the teeming masses around the world who still to hear about Christ or need the Scriptures in their language, etc. It's good to be reminded that such needs still very much exist.

For ministries, publishing gives its leaders the power to share the organization's purpose and vision. I don't mean "vision" in a business buzzword hokey way, that pretentious sounding capital-V *Vision* sort of way. I mean telling the story of what God is doing in and through your organization in a compelling way, chapter by chapter, page by page, story by story. The power to partner through publishing is the ability to stoke a fire in the bosom of your readers. Hopefully, by the time they get to the end of your book, their hearts are warmed to what God is doing through the ministry, and they will want to know more. The book starts that conversation. The conversation starts the relationship. The relationship starts the partnership.

I mentioned you should tell the story of your ministry in a compelling way. I chose that word intentionally. There is compelling storytelling and manipulative storytelling. In sharing what God is doing, as Christians, we must not do it the way the world does. We want to motivate our readers to partner with us, not manipulate them.

The world knows how to tug at heart strings. The world knows how to craft a story to elicit the desired emotional response. We've all seen it. Tender piano and other instrumental playing in a minor key while black-and-white shots of sad people draw you in and prepare you for the appeal. Then the concerned voiceover begins, "For less than the price of a cup a coffee each day, you can help. . ." Regrettably, Christian organizations can sometimes employ the same, well, *ploys*.

Humanly speaking, our Lord did everything contrary to the world's methods of partner-building. He did not court those who had the power and prestige. He alienated them. When crowds got zealous and were ready to make Him king, He withdrew. When they found His teachings too hard and turned away, He didn't change His tack or try to stop them. Even now, everything the Lord does to build His church is 180 degrees opposite of what the world would do. The very message of the gospel is both Good News and the offence of the cross.

Instead of the world's way, we can share our partnership stories with the unique enthusiasm and hopefulness only found the joy of the Lord and the hope of the gospel. We call tell our stories with a glad excitement the world does not have. We can boast of God's goodness. We can boast of His providence—what He has done and what He is doing. If you are helping the abused or needy, don't dwell on where they are; focus on where God has taken those who have come through your doors. He rescues all His children from the trash heap to sit among princes, setting the lonely in families (Ps. 113:7-9). The world would focus on the trash heap. Believers exult in the God who mercifully rescued sinners from there, cleaned them up, adopted them, and brought them into His home to feast at His table! Christian partnership appeals should look and feel different from the world's because, in Christ, we *are* different.

Three elements you can communicate to partners and potential partners are these: Passion, Need, and Urgency.

What is it about your ministry that you are passionate about? Maybe you love what you do because you see lives changed by the power of the gospel. Maybe it is seeing new believers get baptized. Maybe it is the joy in the faces of those believers around the world who benefit from the ministry you lead. When you write, describing your passion for what God is doing, it will show on every page. That passion can inspire and motivate others to come alongside and partner with you.

What does your ministry need? Money is obvious, but what else? What will it need in ten or twenty years? What skills are you looking for in staff you bring on? What about those you serve? What are their needs?

Some ministries choose to operate on a faith basis, making their needs known only to the Lord. If that is your ministry's conviction, there are still plenty of other things you can communicate in a centerpiece book about your ministry. Instead of talking about your ministry's needs, you can talk about the needs of the population you serve. Whatever their need, your ministry centerpiece book can advocate for them.

What is the urgency that drives your ministry? Why? What are the complexities of the situation? The dangers? The political or regional obstacles? Are windows of opportunity opening or closing? Your partners, or your potential partners, may not be aware of any urgency.

For example, before I signed on to go to Burundi, I was unaware of all that the country has gone through. I knew, for instance, about the genocide in Rwanda, but never knew that the same thing was happening in Burundi during that same era. Although both countries have been independent since gaining their freedoms from Belgium in 1962, Burundi has struggled with decades of turmoil and has only had a relative peace for the last few years. Spiritually, Burundi, like many African nations, is also awash in the false teaching of the prosperity gospel. The people there urgently need prayer and training for pastors, as well as for other needs.

Ministries and their leaders can convey the needs and the urgency as a centerpiece book that is a give-away on their website to inform Christians and invite partners.

Opportunities to get involved are part of how God gives us purpose. How did I get to go to Africa the first time? A guest speaker came and preached at our church and invited anyone willing to go with him to Uganda. So, I did. How did I get to go the second time? I had lunch with Johnny Touchet, the head of church-planting ministry, Partner1015 (partner1015.org), and he asked if I wanted to go to Burundi and Uganda. So, I did. Looking back over my years as a believer, every opportunity I have had to become a partner came by invitation.

Think back over your experiences. Sound familiar? Publishing for Christ is the power to partner in written form. It's not an invitation from a pulpit or over lunch, but it is your connection with the reader through the power of the written word—the power of *your* written words, to be exact.

Your book inviting others to partner in what God is doing is important because it can be the vehicle by which God gives someone a newfound sense of purpose. A bored widower who feels himself alone and purposeless can be reinvigorated with the enthusiasm of a mighty Caleb, eighty-four years young and charging to take the hill! Your book could stoke a ministry of vital prayer for someone who is homebound but has hours to intercede for a ministry like yours.

What if you gave copies of your book away to a whole Sunday school class? You may inspire the members to adopt your ministry as their annual cause to rally around and do a service project for.

Parents teach their children the importance of giving by sending a portion of their birthday money to the children helped through your ministry.

Besides giving purpose, partnering can produce bonds of friendship. Depending on the type and size of the ministry, deepening those partnerships can lead to lifelong relationships. My wife and I have co-hosted a podcast in the past. It gave us an opportunity to foster relationships we otherwise would not have had. Partnering is not just about breadth, but depth. Depending upon their expertise, your partners may have insights or connections that God brings alongside your ministry at just the right time.

What if, when you meet someone for coffee to present your plans to go to the mission field, you had a booklet to tell your story and your calling? Your book could talk about the people you hope to serve and what your role will be. Even a book of 10,000 words (about one third of the length of this book) could provide value to your prospective donor. You could also either write that book or a second book and use it for fundraising at the churches you speak at, or simply chalk it up as your own investment to say *thank you* to your supporters.

What if you did not just give your potential support partner one copy of your book, but an extra one to give away to another potential donor he could put you in touch with? Your book passing into the right hands could lead to exciting and divinely appointed opportunities.

Whether you are a solo person in ministry, a family heading off to the mission field, or the leader of a medium to large ministry, publishing a book about what you do is a great way to tap into the power to partner.

If you have a gospel work that is dear to your heart, write about it and share it with the world, and ask the Lord to raise up co-laborers in the work. Publishing can be an exciting way to accelerate the momentum. Those providential partnerships can be personally transformative for your readers, and for you.

Perhaps you are a ministry leader, "the face of the ministry," as it were. A significant part of your role is to meet with current and potential supporters. A book can outline the vision and work of the ministry, with reports of what God has done and is doing in the lives of the men and women and children your ministry serves. And, again, it can make a great ministry gift.

Partnering to Publish-as-Missions

Lastly, publishing a book does cost money. To do it right can be an investment of several thousand dollars. Depending on the size of the ministry, that can come from the ministry's annual marketing budget. If it is just you, or you are part of a smaller ministry, we previously also looked at the idea of funding a publishing project like one would fund a short-term missions trip as one possible way to make it happen. As the saying goes, *Where God guides, God provides.* Rest assured, if the Lord is in the idea, He will provide for your book to see the light of day.

No matter what vocation God has called each of us to, every Christian is called to be a co-laborer in gospel ministry—a Great Commission partner. Why not be a partner in publishing-as-missions?

I mentioned this when we talked about publishing for Christ and the Power to Reach, but it is worth repeating: For the Christian writer who is hindered from going to the mission field, the book can become a sort of missionary. It may sound strange at first, but I see no difference at all in someone raising thousands of dollars to go on a short-term mission trip and someone raising the same amount to publish a solidly useful evangelistic or discipleship-focused book.

Sometimes (not always), the investment in the book may actually make more sense than going. For one thing, you might be too old, or your health might not be suited for the mission field. Or maybe God has you at home raising the children and they are your mission field at this stage of your life. Making the time and having the discipline to write one quality book may do more and go farther than you physically could go at this stage of your life.

Another reason it may make sense to help finance "sending a book" instead is this: A quality book can endure for decades. Or it can be revised and given new life periodically. Either way, the initial investment produces a work that can literally span generations. Imagine, as an author, writing a book that your great-grandchildren will read.

Can you imagine the eternal dividends of investing in a gospel-publishing initiative? Who knows how the Lord may choose to use it!

Frankly, one reason I am excited about writing *this* book because it is my prayer that the Lord would be pleased to bless it and put it into the hands of someone who publishes for Christ and that person's book (*your book?*) reaches even one soul for Christ (let alone hundreds or thousands). Then I would have a small gospel share in that work. Talk about eternal dividends! Sign me up.

So, I return to the "missions fundraising" thought. Have you ever contributed to send a church member on a short-term mission trip? Sure you have. Has your church ever held a missions fundraiser? Surely it has. Why not have a "missions fund raiser" to raise funds to help an author in your church self-publish his or her work? Our church did something like this this year.

We have a very talented music leader and elder named Dustin Meadows. Dustin writes and records his own worship songs (DustinMeadowsMusic.com). This year he had the desire to record another CD of original songs for his next album. The church made everyone aware of the project and created a dedicated giving account towards it. Money was raised and the album was produced—and it is fantastic! I am honored that the donation my wife and I contributed to the project helped in some small way.

In fact, when I went to Africa later in the year, I brought over a few of Dustin's songs, with a few of them translated into French. I don't know how many churches may be using his songs, but I know I shared them with quite a few pastors over Whatsapp. Dustin's songs were the missionary. He published for Christ and used the power to partner.

How else can you partner, or ask others to partner

with you in publishing? Well, do you know two or more languages? I mean really know them? You can partner to translate someone else's book for them, or check the translation. Can you edit? You can help a writer edit his or her manuscript. Like to read? How about offering to be a beta-reader (someone volunteers to be a pre-publication reader, offering constructive feedback). Have an eye for graphics? You can help design an eye-catching cover or help with any needed illustrations inside. Whatever talents God has given you, I am sure there is a need for them in publishing for Christ.

I hope you see the potential in the power to partner and are excited both to get partners and to be one for someone else.

9

The Power
to Tear Down and
Build Up

Solomon knew a thing or two about building. The Lord used him to build the Temple, the royal palace, stables for his thousands of horses, and many other building projects. No wonder, then, that when he writes of the times and seasons for everything in life, he adds that there is **a time to tear down and a time to build** (Eccl. 3:3). This chapter is about how we can use words and ideas to pull down wrong things and build right things, to the glory of God and the benefit of our readers.

The Power to Tear Down

My wife and I moved to South Carolina nearly a decade ago. In our town, there stood a blush-red brick Colonial-style farmhouse my wife liked to admire whenever we drove by. It was two stories tall, rectangular, and flanked by chimneys at either end, with a craftsman-style covered porch added on the front sometime later. All sitting elegantly behind a low, black, wrought-iron fence. It was stiffly formal yet also quaint and homey—one of the last local remnants of a time a couple generations ago when this area was nothing but farmland. It was beautiful in its simplicity. The story is such a familiar one that you already know where it is going.

One day we drove by and mourned when we saw a yard full of utility flags and survey stakes ominously dotting the property. Another time we drove by, all the trees were cut down. The fateful day eventually came. That picturesque home of a bygone era was reduced to a heap. Bummer. The house was probably in need of costly repairs and the land was probably worth more than the house. But still. Bummer.[19]

By contrast, there are other times when a thing is so vile it needs to be wiped off the face of the earth. Solomon also said, **"A wise man scales the city of the mighty and pulls down the stronghold in which they trust,"** using metaphor to urge the wise to tear down the lofty ideas of the foolish and the evil (Prov. 21:22). A couple of years ago, on the other side of town, a strip club next to the highway was shut down. Eventually, a church moved into the vacant commercial space. Good riddance and praise the Lord.

Earlier, we looked at scenes from the life of Gideon. We saw in Judges 6:24 that Gideon **"built an altar to the LORD there. . ."** Gideon would soon build another altar. But Gideon knew a thing or two about tearing down as well. Right after he built that altar, the Lord told him to tear down the altar to the demon god Baal that his father had erected, as well as the profane Asherah pole next to it. Once the altar was demolished, Gideon was to build

---

19 Writing this chapter, I had the idea to look for it online. Sadly, it was even prettier and more picturesque than I remembered. At least it is preserved in photos. https://maps.app.goo.gl/ DFb9EcRuJyYDnZTLA.

an altar to the true God, the LORD, where it stood, and offer a sacrifice to the LORD on it (Judges 6:25-27). Despite fearing the townspeople and obeying under cover of darkness, by first light the deed was done. Good riddance and praise the Lord.

Gideon is not the only divinely appointed demolitions expert.

Emboldened Peter did this at Pentecost. He told the Jewish leaders that the believers were not drunk as they, the leaders, supposed, quoted Joel to put the event in its prophesied context, and then he preached Christ (Acts 2:14-40). After his and John's arrest for preaching Christ, the Jewish leaders commanded them to stop, but Peter and John weren't having it. Instead, they courageously declared, **"Judge for yourselves whether it is right in God's sight to listen to you rather than God. For we cannot stop speaking about what we have seen and heard"** (Acts 4:19-20).

Stephen sealed his testimony of Christ with his life. A mob of religious Jews attacked him as he preached Christ. Luke records this:

> **But resistance arose from what was called the Synagogue of the Freedmen, including Cyrenians, Alexandrians, and men from the provinces of Cilicia and Asia. They began to argue with Stephen, but they could not stand up to his wisdom or the Spirit by whom he spoke.**
> **(Acts 6:9-10)**

Stephen was dragged before the Jewish Council and a

mob trial took place, climaxing in his stoning. They may have destroyed his body, but not before he called out their religious hypocrisy and leveled their self-righteousness.

Paul was also an ideological demolitions expert. In Acts 17, at the Aeropagus in Athens, he quoted a secular poet as an inroad to tearing down their erroneous ideologies and exposing their idols. Then he preached the true and living Christ. He would do it again in his letter to the Galatians, tearing down the folly of going back to rely on works of the Law to save.

Consider also Paul's words to the Corinthians:

> **For though we live in the flesh, we do not wage war according to the flesh. The weapons of our warfare are not the weapons of the world. Instead, they have divine power to demolish strongholds. We tear down arguments and every presumption set up against the knowledge of God. . .**
> **(2 Cor. 10:3-5a)**

The application here for us is that we are to be busy doing the same thing. As truth bearers, we Christians are to refute the erroneous arguments and ideas of our day with gospel truth. Remember Paul's charge to Timothy:

> **All Scripture is God-breathed and is useful for instruction, for conviction, for correction, and for training in righteousness, so that the man of God may be complete, fully equipped for every good work.**
> **(2 Tim. 3:16-17)**

When we appeal to Scripture, you and I bring its truths to bear in teaching, reproving, correcting, and training against all that stands in opposition to the cause of Christ. This happens when a Christian college student stands up for Christ in the face of mockery and scorn of his or her God-hating professor. Or when godly parents stand courageously for Christ and the safety of their children against a perverse school board. Whenever you engage in a conversation with a lost person, fielding questions and refuting challenges, you are working to demolish their errant belief system, hoping the Lord will replace it with the gospel of truth.

Writing and publishing give us the same opportunities to tear down arguments and godless ideologies. Someone once wrote, "The pen is mightier than the sword." Earlier we heard from Ernest Reisinger in his essay, *Every Christian a Publisher*. He reminds us that, "the pen has been the hammer to break the errors of centuries."[20] Yes, it does.

The world desperately needs to be shown the eternal misery that exists and awaits behind all that it holds dear. By the Spirit's empowering, your words can have that effect for someone. One person may not sound like much, but think of the precious value of that eternal soul!

Look around. Look at the world around us. Look at the messages people have on their sweatshirts. Self is exalted. Vulgarity is exalted. The profane is now sacred and the sacred is now profane. Very little in society remains off limits. Human life is worthless in the womb and cheap on the streets. It only has value when it can bring profit by being trafficked. Look at what is valued versus what is

20 https://graceonlinelibrary.org/salvation/evangelism/every-christian-a-publisher-by-earnest-c-reisinger/

despised in our society. Relativism, sexual confusion, and deviancy are exalted, while all that God declares is vehemently rejected.

When you and I "tear-down for Christ," we join Gideon, Peter, John, Stephen, Paul, and the great cloud of witnesses who have gone before us destroying altars and idols and replacing them with the Good News of the Lord Jesus Christ, **"who is God over all, forever worthy of praise! Amen"** (Rom. 9:5).

Tearing down the idols our culture worships is God-honoring. Smashing the edifice of dead religion, self-exaltation, rebellion against the things and Person of God. . . . Those glorify God. To put it another way, it's breaking up the fallow ground. The tiller must get underneath the hard-packed soil, upsetting and overturning the whole field. If he doesn't, the field remains unproductive, yielding only grass and weeds instead of an abundant, healthy harvest of fruits, vegetables, or grain.

At times, tearing down is the only option. The roof is collapsed, the beams are destroyed, and the frame is compromised beyond repair. It's a danger to be in. Time to tear it down.

But Christians are not iconoclasts for the sport of it. We don't go around smashing the idols of someone's beliefs because it's provocative or fun. Rather, true Christians do what they do because they are motivated by love. We love our Lord, and we love the soul in front of us who is alienated from Him and on whom His wrath thus abides (John 3:36). We don't tear down with words of anger but with words of conviction, authority, and love. We Christians have the opportunity to plead through publishing that men and women abandon their broken cisterns, turn to the Lord, and be saved.

The Word of God tears me down daily. Each day when I read the Word, I am leveled at the reminder of some sin, some quality in my heart that needs to be torn down. And I thank God for it. God has used the godly writings of countless men and women over the years to do the same thing. Godly writers can tie a rope of words around the idols we have erected in our lives and bring them smashing to the ground. Selfishness. Covetousness. Lust. Anger. Only as the plume of dust rises do we finally see the rubble of our prayerlessness. Our lovelessness. Our impatience. The list goes on. And just when one idol gets torn down, in our flesh we habitually raise another, and then the entire process has to be repeated until the Lord takes us home. Good riddance and praise the Lord.

The Power to Build Up

If only we tear down idols, we leave the job half done. Something else, better, needs be built in its place. The only structure that belongs over the rubble and remnants is an altar to the Lord. Publishing for Christ also carries with it the power to build up, to edify, one's readers. By "building up," I mean giving correct doctrine, guiding as to correct biblical behavior, and teaching our readers discernment. We might say that this corresponds to the phrase in the Great Commission, where Jesus said, ". . .**teaching them to obey all that I have commanded you**" (Matt. 28:20). Tearing down and building up helps others to mature because it teaches them to know, love, and obey Jesus more.

Just how important is the power to build up? To answer

that, we need to take a closer look at Paul's words in 1 Corinthians 14. To set the scene for us, you remember that Paul first begins to discuss spiritual gifts in Chapter 12. Then, in Chapter 13, he famously and beautifully urges the Corinthian Christians to love. In Chapter 14, he returns to instructing them about the gifts. In those opening verses, he urges them to **"earnestly pursue love and eagerly desire spiritual gifts, especially the gift of prophecy"** (1 Cor. 14:1). The gift of prophecy was not just about foretelling future events; the word used also refers to "a person gifted at expositing divine truth"[21]—that is, to be able to prophecy means having the ability to teach sound doctrine.

Paul builds his case by listing three reasons why prophecy is better than tongues. Those who prophecy can edify, encourage, and comfort individuals (v. 3). In the next verse, he expands his argument, adding that prophecy **"edifies the church"**(v. 4). In verse twelve, he again emphasizes this ability to build up when he says, **"Strive to excel in gifts that build up the church."** I find both halves of this exhortation to be interesting. First, **"strive to excel in"** means to diligently seek to be super-abounding in. Paul's exhortation to the believers is one of vivid words and pictures painted using a wide brush! And what exactly were the Corinthian Christians—and, by application, you and me—supposed to diligently seek to be super-abundant in? **"Gifts that build up the church."**

Paul then offers a practical application: he tells them that if he had to choose, he would rather speak just five words of instruction that could be plainly understood

21 Prophecy comes from the root "prophétés." See Strong's 4396, https://bible-hub.com/greek/4396.htm.

than ten thousand words in an incomprehensible tongue (v. 19). (Incidentally, is there any clearer argument for the importance of clearly communicating to your audience?)

All of this helps us understand how important the power to build up is. You and I are to strive to overflowingly abound in this gift of clearly and accurately teaching God's Word to build up, encourage, and comfort individuals and build up the Church.

Proverbs 15:14 says, "A discerning heart seeks knowledge, but the mouth of a fool feeds on folly." Discernment (or "understanding") takes initiative. Tenacity. The Hebrew word there for "seek" has with it the connotation of straining after the thing sought. Striving. The discerning heart wants to get to the truth, and the person with a discerning heart will dig and dig until arriving at the truth.

Foolish people are not going to make the effort. That is not to say they don't seek out any information at all. They may be diligent in other areas of their life. Oftentimes people are diligent in seeking knowledge in the things of this world, like their career field or their financial investments, but they take spiritual false teaching at face value and lose their soul (Mark 8:36). That makes their folly even more tragic. I have known, and I am sure you have as well, many bright, intelligent people with advanced degrees, but they are devotees of a false religion or a well-known religious cult. They have brilliant minds, but they feed their eternal souls on folly.

God's Word informs us that every person already knows the truth, but chooses to suppress it (Rom. 1:18). Paul goes on in that passage to use the same word as in Proverbs 15:14, that in the end, those who claim to be wise become, as the New Living Translation emphasizes it, **"utter"** fools (Rom. 1:22, NLT). Publishing for Christ gives us an opportunity to tear down idols and lovingly confront people with the truth.

Tragically, lack of discernment is rife among professing believers, too. The American health-and-wealth prosperity "gospel" continues to wreak havoc wherever it is exported around the world. For all its emotion and Bible quoting, it presents nothing more than a shallow, materialistic, syncretized blending of twisted Bible passages, shamanism, and animism. Instead of taking your offering to the village witch doctor to get your healing, you take your money to the "church" with the charismatic pastor who, in exchange, mesmerizes with Bible verses out of context, promising abundant blessing and healing. And all around the world people continue to consume it.

I am reminded of Paul's word to the Christians at Colossae. He did not say they would get led astray by obvious error. Rather, he warned them to beware of being deceived by the ones that sounded **"plausible"** (Col. 2:4 ESV). The men in 2 Kings 4 knew right away there was something wrong with their lunch. **"When they tasted the stew they cried out, "There is death in the pot, O man of God!" And they could not eat it."** Plausible false teaching is not that obvious. It tastes fine going down but turns out to be deadly poison.

When I was in Africa this last time, I saw roadside vendors selling white, woven baskets to be used in churches as offering baskets. Some were simply labeled with the word OFFERING on the side. Others were labeled with the telltale money euphemism of the prosperity gospel,

SEED. Plausible, but poison!

Every believer is charged to exercise discernment. Jesus commanded it. "**Watch out no one leads you astray**" (Matt. 24:4, NIV). The apostle John said, "**Test the spirits**" (1 John 4:1) and Paul charged, "**See to it that no one takes you captive through philosophy and empty deception, which are based on human tradition and the spiritual forces of the world rather than on Christ**" (Col. 2:8). Publishing for Christ, we can help our brothers and sisters in Christ to be discerning, like others have helped us. What an opportunity before us to build up others for their good and for God's glory.

10

The Power
to Lift Up

In the last chapter, we talked about Christian publishing's power to tear down and build up—that dismantling of wrong ideas and false teaching and erecting sound doctrine over the rubble. In this chapter, we'll consider the power to lift up, that is, the power to encourage.

Coming Alongside with Hope

Despite the decline of personal letter writing and the ever-increasing cost of a postage stamp, the global greeting card industry in 2022 was valued at over 19 billion dollars. People still enjoy the goodwill feeling of sending and receiving cards and notes of encouragement.

And that speaks to the power of encouragement. Even the secular world understands what it means to the human spirit to be encouraged. Cheered. Buoyed. Lifted up (even if people wouldn't necessarily use that phrase).

Oftentimes, cards and notes are the last mementos we have of loved ones who are no longer with us. In a drawer in my office, I have a bundle of old cards. Many are from my mother and my father and his second wife, all of whom are gone now. They are a powerful connection. They are echoes of the past, my beloved parents expressing their love for me, their son. They shopped for every card; took time to find just the right one; took a moment to think of just the right words to say in it; and then took a few minutes to seal, stamp, and send it. And now those drugstore greeting cards are precious heirlooms.

Already we can see how important it is for human beings to have a sense of hope, to be encouraged. This also reminds us that words matter. People can be moved by the words they read—so much so that the words we write today can be treasured by friends and loved ones long after we're gone.

Author and speaker John Lehman knows a thing or two about encouragement. In his book *Encouragement: Refreshing Others with a Word Fitly Spoken,* Lehman explains that the New Testament Greek word for encouragement, *paraklesis,* is a composite of two words meaning "alongside of" and "to call." He notes: "When people come alongside us during difficult times to give us renewed courage, a renewed spirit, renewed hope, that's true encouragement."[22]

I can tell you from personal experience, John practices what he preaches! He was my and my wife's supervisor/mentor for our last push to get our biblical counseling certifications. If it were not for his ongoing words of "renewed hope" urging us to keep going, neither of us would've crossed the finish line.

Encouragement is also kindness in action. In my brief

22   John Lehman. *Encouragement: Refreshing Others with a Word Fitly Spoken,* GreatWriting.org, page 89.

time working in real estate, I was always writing and sending note cards. Yes, it was good business, but I also genuinely enjoyed writing to various people to let them know they were on my mind. I always tried to highlight something about them I appreciated or was thankful for. People were often surprised to receive a sincere and handwritten card.

Even today, although I have moved to sending text messages, I still enjoy dropping a joke to someone as a way of saying hi, or telling a brother that I am praying for him. I think it makes that person's day a little brighter. It shows someone thinks about them. Someone cares enough to mention them by name to the Father. We all need that from time to time.

Long before Job was known for his suffering, his friends loved and esteemed him for being an encourager. **"Surely you have instructed many, and have strengthened their feeble hands. Your words have steadied those who stumbled; you have braced the knees that were buckling"** (Job 4:3-4). What a powerful endorsement. What a godly testimony to the power of one man's words to do good to so many. A few years ago, when the significance of these verses first hit me, I penciled a note in the margin of my Bible next to them. Ever since, whenever I reread this passage, I am challenged anew by those three simple words I wrote off to the side: *Be like Job*. How can your words instruct, strengthen, steady, and brace those who are feeble, stumbling, and buckling under the pressures of life? How can you *be like Job*?

If you're not in the habit of being an encourager, let me commend it to you. I am sure you already know this, but as you encourage others, the Lord blesses you with a little bit of joy in return.

It's easy to get weary in this world, isn't it? Day after day we feel the effects of the fall all around us. Paul talked about how we, along with the whole of creation, groan under the weight of it all (Rom. 8:22-23). That weariness can lead to discouragement.

Discouragement is an awful feeling. The heaviness; the foreboding sense of hopelessness in the moment; that pit-in-your-stomach feeling when there is simply no wind left in your sails. Discouragement leads to sadness, the kind that turns to gloom and feels heavier every day. Just as being cold and damp can lead to a case of pneumonia, left untreated a bitter draft of discouragement can knock us down for the count with depression and despair. Encouragement is what lifts us up. Encouragement revives us.

Proverbs 15:23 says **"A man takes joy in a fitting reply—and how good is a timely word!"** What a blessing a word in season is to the discouraged heart—what a ray of sunshine breaking into someone's gray, overcast world. Sadness dissipates and cheerfulness—what only a short time ago seemed too good to ever be true again—breaks and rises upon the heart's horizon.

And truly *biblical* encouragement diffuses the fragrance of Christ, stirring spirit and soul like nothing and no one else can. That is why we need more believers publishing hope-filled words that lift up their readers, taking them under their arm and escorting them gently to the Savior.

I like the way the King James Version translates Romans 10:15b, "**How beautiful are the feet of them that preach the gospel of peace, and bring glad tidings of good things!**" The sentence itself is uplifting. Like an array of jewels in a setting, look at the words all clustered together: "gospel," "peace," "glad tidings," and "good things."

This is one of those verses full of the fragrance of distinctly Christian virtues. For all the many beautiful things men and women can write, there are no sentiments as beautiful as the ones expressing Christian virtues. Look in all the writings of the world's religions or any secular literature, and you won't find it. It doesn't exist. There is no good news like the gospel. There is no peace like what is brought by the Prince of Peace.

One day in 2018 when I was still in real estate, a man stopped into the office to see me, but I was not in at the time. Our office manager told me about him the next time I was in the office.

The man said he was passing through town and wanted to meet me. Since I wasn't in, he asked the receptionist for a piece of paper to leave me a note, which she then handed to me. I thought he was interested in buying or selling a house.

To my surprise, it was one of the nicest notes I have ever received. He had read a devotional booklet I wrote for a ministry and just wanted to come in and thank me for what I had written.

It's amazing to think that this event happened six years ago, and yet his one kind act of encouragement lives on. Not only am I now telling you the story of his encouragement, but his handwritten note remains tacked to the corkboard in my office. I am looking at it now.

That brother wanted to tell me how much my words encouraged him, but little did he know how much his note of encouragement lifted *me* up. Isn't that so often how the Body of Christ functions?

It's in the Job Description

About AD50, Paul wrote his first letter to the church at Thessalonica. The church was young and needed some nurturing. Toward the end of his brief letter Paul wrote:

> **For God has not appointed us to suffer wrath, but to obtain salvation through our Lord Jesus Christ. He died for us so that, whether we are awake or asleep, we may live together with Him. Therefore encourage and build one another up, just as you are already doing.**
> **(1 Thess. 5:9-11)**

Paul exhorts them to continue to "encourage" and "build one another up." The word "encourage" there is a compound word meaning "with counsel, advice." We believers are to be busy encouraging one another with words of counsel, "constructing" each other up in the Lord. What a beautiful picture of how we are to be toward each other.

But even more beautiful is the reason or impetus behind it all. Verse eleven begins with the word "Therefore." As the pastor who married me and Amy used to say, "Whenever we see a 'therefore,' we have to stop and ask what the 'therefore' is there for." Look at verses nine and ten. Because of the work of the gospel, God's electing mercy, Christ's vicarious atoning death, and the life we now have in Him. . . . Because of those glorious reasons, we are to be encouraging and building one another up in the Lord to press on, to enjoy the full salvation that is ours in Christ.

In the letter to the Hebrews, the author commands that we are to check our own hearts for sin or anything displeasing to the Lord (Heb. 3:12). Then, we are to encourage one another "every day" so that none of us gets hardened hearts because of sin's powers to deceive (Heb. 3:13).

Over the years, I have looked at a lot of job descriptions. Job descriptions, if you've never worked in the corporate world, are just that: The details of the role, its responsibilities, the required skills, and the overall qualifications. It's not an exhaustive list. There's usually a catch-all phrase at the bottom, like "And other duties as assigned." In the roles and responsibilities of a Christian, we are to be lifting up one another. Encouragement is in the job description!

Think again of our Lord. Jesus was a burden-lifter. Everywhere He went, He took upon Himself the burdens of others. His title of The Suffering Servant wasn't just about His passion. His whole blessed incarnation involved being a servant. Now we, too, are called to serve. We Christians are called to be burden-lifters to those around us.

Samuel Rutherford (1600-1661) was a Scottish pastor who was eventually jailed and exiled to Aberdeen for two years for his faith. In exile, he corresponded with his parishioners and friends, some of whom were even members of the nobility. Despite having to endure his own great trial, Rutherford spent his time writing hundreds of such letters. Only a few years after his death, his letters, warm and overflowing with the encouragements of the Savior, were gathered and published. They have never gone out of print. They are one of the greatest, if not *the* greatest, examples of publishing for Christ and the power to lift up that we have outside of the Scriptures.

There will likely never be another volume of encouragements to Christians like the *Letters of Samuel Rutherford*. But should someone who loves to sculpt or paint give it up because of not being another Michelangelo? Should I give up guitar because I am not another Andrés Segovia? What matters to the Lord is not the greatness of what we do, but our love and devotion to Him. Look at what the Lord did with a boy's five loaves of bread and two fish.

One person may try to read Rutherford's letters and struggle to get anything out of them. But then that person might read your book (or blog, or hear your song or podcast, or audiobook) and that can be what the Lord uses to urge her on in her walk with Jesus.

You can encourage the downtrodden. You can write a book that causes someone to get to the end and think, *I really needed that.* Your words may be the words God uses to lift up a weary saint and urge him on in Christ another day. *Your words!*

And you can do it anytime, day or night, anywhere in the world the winds of providence carry your encouraging words. See the potential in this exciting opportunity?

Have you ever faced losing your job? What was it like?

What do you remember of how you felt? What uncertainties? What fearful thoughts preyed upon you? How did the Lord bring about a blessed resolution? There's your book to unburden and encourage the unemployed.

Have you faced suffering? Have you heard those dreaded words from the doctor, "The results came back. It is cancer." Or have you had to walk that dark valley with a loved one? Can you recall stories of God's grace breaking through on the tough days? What can you say to offer hope to someone who just got the bad news? What empathy can you extend to that person's selfless caregiver? There's your book to unburden and encourage the sick or the caregiver who is trying to keep it all together on the outside but is burdened by discouragement within. Your words of experience, love, and care would do wonders.

If you wonder who could use encouragement, just look around. There are people all around us who could use a kind word to lift the spirits. I am writing this chapter in another coffee shop. It's a coffee shop that also sells ice cream. Even though it is the end of December, the place is a buzz with people. Even in winter, people love ice cream. Something about ice cream puts people in a good mood, doesn't it? Plus, it's the holiday season. Everyone here is talking, smiling, and laughing. It's nice to see.

Still, if you and I were to interview each person privately, I am sure we would find that every one of them is struggling with something. Everybody has some area in his or her life and could use some "walk alongside" time from someone to bring help and cheer along the way—some help carrying their burdens.

We see the need all around us. Now we have to ask: *Lord, How can I help?*

Publishing for Christ is empowering. It empowers us to lift up the downcast, come alongside and support the weak, to speak hope and courage to the one feeling panicked and storm-tossed or hopelessly adrift. Your words can cheer hearts. You can inspire people with reminders that the Lord is sovereign, He is good, and He is in control of whatever trials they are enduring. You can be the one to share Jesus' invitation to weary souls to lay their burdens at His feet and find rest for their souls (Matt. 11:28-30).

Your words could do all of that if you would write and publish them. Will you? Why not scatter seed along the path and trust the Lord for the increase!

I hope that I have again challenged—or should I say, *encouraged* you—to the exciting possibilities when you take the step to be a digital missionary.

11

Conclusion:
The Power to Serve

This is it. The end of the book. Thank you so much for sticking with me until now. In this last chapter, I want to leave you with a few final thoughts to inspire and motivate you to answer the call to labor and serve as a digital missionary. I think Paul's words in 1 Corinthians 15:58 are a good place to get us excited about serving:

> **Therefore, my beloved brothers, be steadfast and immovable. Always excel in the work of the Lord, because you know that your labor in the Lord is not in vain.**

Paul had just spent fifty-seven verses talking about the believer's sure hope of resurrection; because Christ was raised in triumph, we too will be raised. Next, he says, **"Therefore,"** which is to say, "based on everything I just explained." **"Therefore, my beloved brothers,"** notice who Paul is exhorting there. He is not just addressing the elders and deacons, his words are to every believer. That is important for us to think about because that means Paul's charge to them applies to us, too. **"Steadfast and immovable"** are fascinating because commentators say that, taken together, they speak of both inward and outward dogged perseverance. Then Paul lays out the rest of his charge. The ESV says, **"always abounding in the work of the Lord."** I like what Bible commentator Albert Barnes writes about this phrase:

> Always abounding in the work of the Lord—Always engaged in doing the will of God; in promoting his glory, and advancing his kingdom. The phrase means not only to be engaged in this, but to be *engaged diligently, laboriously; excelling* in this. The "work of the Lord" here means that which the Lord requires; all the appropriate duties of Christians. Paul exhorts them to practice every Christian virtue, and *to do all that they could do to further the gospel among people.*[23]

Paul concludes his charge with a wonderful promise, **"knowing that in the Lord your labor is not in vain."** Read that again. God, through Paul, is assuring His people that we can have absolute confidence (**"knowing that"**) that not a single thing we do in this life "to further the gospel among people" (as Barnes puts it) will have been an unfruitful waste of time. Amazing!

I titled this chapter "The Power to Serve" because I hope that you have caught the vision to "go" and been inspired to "serve" on the digital mission field. Now that you

---

23 https://biblehub.com/commentaries/1_corinthians/15-58.htm, emphases added.

are aware of the exciting potential that is literally at your fingertips, my prayer is that you will answer the call to either publish for Christ yourself or help someone else's desire to do so, such as your pastor or a ministry leader you know. You can be a digital missionary serving on the supply chain that keeps them advancing. Buy their books and give them away. Share their blog posts on your social media. Encourage them in their podcasting. And, of course, pray for them and those they seek to reach.

Being a digital missionary is truly a labor (serving) of (motivated by) love. This chapter could have easily been called "The Power to Love" because to serve with a Christlike heart is to do it out of love, and love is demonstrated in serving. As others have said, love is the root and serving is the fruit. How can I say I love my wife if I never do things to demonstrate my love, like speak kindly, ask forgiveness, take out the trash, or help in other ways that keep our household in working order? Serving is where the rubber meets the road. If we're loving, it will show in our serving.

As I write, I don't know who will read this book. But I am thinking of Christian young people, students, young-marrieds, professionals and tradespeople, and lost people, too. Who of them may be served by what you write or produce? Who might go to a mission field? Who might become a chaplain? A nurse? A pastor? Who might stop abusing his or her spouse? Who might read your words and finally quit drinking and drugs, and call on the name of the Lord?

On and on the possibilities go. Have you seen them? Are you convinced of them?

I am praying for this book. I am praying God would use it to put on your heart a desire to publish something for God's glory. That is why I am also praying for your book— praying that your words or your willingness to partner to publish someone else's words, will, in turn, serve others.

One of my favorite examples in the Bible of service is Peter's mother-in-law. Although she's only mentioned once in passing in Scripture, her story is included all three synoptic Gospels. Here is Mark's account of her story:

> **Simon's mother-in-law was sick in bed with a fever, and they promptly told Jesus about her. So He went to her, took her by the hand, and helped her up. The fever left her, and she began to serve them. (Mark 1:30-31)**

Here's what I once wrote about this passage:

> Every time I read this story, it makes me stop. So typical of God's word, two sentences of text give us more wisdom and insight than others could write in a whole book. The Lord healed Peter's mother-in-law and when she rose from her sickbed what did she do? She served them.
>
> This is exactly what God does in the life of every believer. God heals us—actually, raises us from our dead, sinful state—so we can rise and serve. We serve God by serving others, exactly like Scripture shows Peter's mother-in-law doing. It is a beautiful exchange: out of death's uselessness the Spirit of God brings life and usefulness.

What are some things in your life that Jesus healed you from? Drugs? Pornography? Greed? Abuse? One day all whom the Lord has healed from sin and death will be in heaven sharing what he has done, and how he used them. Jesus has healed you to serve. I can't wait to hear your story![24]

All of us ought to strive to serve like Peter's mother-in-law. You and I have also been "healed to serve." How can your words, your testimony of God's grace and mercy in your life, serve others? You may never actually know the full answer on this side of eternity. What an exciting and God-glorifying possibility!

No discussion of the power to love and serve others is complete without looking to the Lord Jesus, whose whole incarnational life and atoning death were love on display through serving.

> **So He got up from the supper, laid aside His outer garments, and wrapped a towel around His waist. After that, He poured water into a basin and began to wash the disciples' feet and dry them with the towel that was around Him.**
> **(John 13:4-5)**

We Christians, as new creations, are divinely empowered to do many things. For example: We can pray fervently and effectively, we can resist temptation, and we can gladly give up our own reputations to serve others,

---

24   Anthony Russo. *Pleasant Places: Reflections on the Christian Life*, 2021. Mark520.org.

all for the glory of God. In short: We have a new will and are Spirit-enabled to deny ourselves and seek to serve like Jesus modeled for us. The power to serve our generation (and beyond) through all of the modern avenues of technology that are available is a remarkable opportunity the Lord gives us.

The Power to Testify One Last Time

This may be the conclusion of this book but think about the conclusion of your own life. If you had one last opportunity to address humanity, what would you say?

When I can't speak anymore, I am excited to go to my eternal joy knowing that my "loaves and fishes" evangelistic book *Jesus Changed Everything* will continue to herald the glories of the Lord Jesus Christ for me!

The opportunity for you to be a digital missionary and publish for Christ is an opportunity to stand before the world, as it were, and say something. What would you say? Seize the opportunity!

By the time this book is published, I'll turn fifty-three. Time has flown by. I can't believe I am in my fifties. Not a day goes by that I don't think about how little time I have left for Christ. Luther Rice died at fifty-three. What if it were my year, too? Because I often think about the brevity of life, let me share some thought-provoking, inspiring stories with you:

On Saturday, September 29, 1770, the great evangelist George Whitefield, weak, sick, and knowing his time was short, preached one last time. He was helped onto a barrel as he traveled to a preaching engagement and preached an impromptu sermon to the crowd that had gathered around his coach to see him. Strengthened by God, he preached for two hours. That night, his sleep was broken as he labored to breathe because of his asthma. Some of his last-known words were, "I would rather wear out than rust out." By the next morning he did just that as he passed into glory.

Some readers may be old enough to remember the name Paul E. Little. Little worked for InterVarsity Christian Fellowship for a quarter century and was professor of evangelism at Trinity Evangelical Divinity School in Deerfield, Illinois. He is probably most remembered for his book, *How to Give Away Your Faith*. Little died suddenly in 1975 at just forty-six years of age.

His wife, Marie, would spend the rest of her life updating his books, compiling new ones from recorded material, and keeping his ministry going. She explained her reticence about doing that, and what (or who) inspired her to overcome it, in the Preface to the updated version of *Give Away*:

> One discovery helped to dispel the fears and inadequacies I felt about this undertaking. I learned that every one of Oswald Chambers's prolific writings were published posthumously. During his lectures between 1907 and 1917, his wife took shorthand notes from which all of his books were produced after his death in his early forties. Paul was in his late forties when an automobile accident took him to heaven while our family was on vacation. There are some obvious parallels in our two stories. I took this widow's model as the Lord's prompting to undertake this update. . .[25]

25   Paul E. Little, *How to Give Away Your Faith,* IVP Books, Downers Grove, Illinois
Pages 14-15

God used these godly women to honor their husbands' legacies and publish for Christ, and countless saints have been blessed by their faithful co-labors. I have also already mentioned how the world has been blessed by the editing and publishing efforts of Jonathan Edwards to publish his missionary son-in-law David Brainerd's journals.

Writing takes discipline, but so does anything that is worth doing. "Our work is great," Puritan Thomas Watson said, "Our time short, and our Master urgent."

Finally, C.E. Orr brings words together beautifully when he talks about the difference you and I can make in the world if we so choose:

> The literal translation of 2 Cor. 2:14 reads thus: "But thanks be to God, who leads me on from place to place in the train of his triumph, to celebrate his victory over the enemies of Christ, and by me sends forth the knowledge of him, a stream of fragrant incense, throughout the world." A saintly life diffuses a sweet, heavenly fragrance throughout the world, and brings a knowledge of God and the nature of his salvation to the minds of men. Let me exhort you, therefore, to a pure life, a life full of devotion and reverence to God. You can make your life, by God's grace, a constant, flowing stream of fragrant incense, whose sweetness will linger long on the air after you have passed to higher realms.[26]

Besides the Scriptures themselves, think about the books that have made the greatest impressions on you for Christ. That is the power of the written word. Those writ-

26   C.E. Orr https://ccel.org/ccel/orrce/lambs/lambs.xii.html

ers wrote what they did for all the reasons we've talked about. And, however God has gifted you, you can do this, too. You can play a vital part in getting quality Christian literature and media into the world. The possibilities have never been more affordable or more available.

I have pleaded my case. The rest is up to you.

Will you be a digital missionary?

About Anthony Russo

For twenty years Anthony Russo was a nominal cultural Christian. That is, until September 2005 when the Lord soundly saved him. "I really am what the Bible calls "born again." I am not who I was, my life and my heart are completely different. Selfishness, guilt, and shame were replaced with a genuine love for God and people. Jesus changed my life. He can change yours, too."

Since then, Anthony has wanted to tell the world about Jesus. He is the author of several 30-day devotionals for *Anchor*, the devotional ministry of Haven Today, numerous blog articles, and now five books including *LOVE, LEAD, SERVE: The Christian Man's Call to Serve His Family and His Church*.

Anthony Russo is the creator and, along with his wife, Amy, co-host of the weekly Christian podcast, Grace and Peace Radio, available on your favorite podcast app, The Christian Podcast Community, The Society of Reformed Podcasters, or at GraceandPeaceRadio.com.

Anthony is completing his doctoral studies (D.Min, Biblical Counseling) at Bob Jones University. He has an MA in Biblical Counseling, a Master of Divinity from Luther Rice College and Seminary, and an MBA from LSU Shreveport. He and Amy are both certified biblical counselors with ACBC and IABC; they live in Greenville, South Carolina.

www.ingramcontent.com/pod-product-compliance
Lightning Source LLC
Chambersburg PA
CBHW050215270326
41914CB00003BA/415